Page 41

Page 42

Page 43

Page 44

Page 45

Page 46

Page 47

Page 48

Page 49

Page 50

Page 51

Page 52

Page 53

Page 54

Page 55

Page 56

Page 57

Page 58

Page 59

Page 60

Parent Signature

Page 61

Page 62

Page 63

Page 64

Page 65

Page 66

Page 67

Page 68

Page 69

Page 70

Parent Signature

Page 71

Page 72

Page 73

Page 74

Page 75

Page 76

Page 77

Page 78

Page 79

Page 80

Concept - Letter A

Find And Color Letter A

Date:__________

A

A

B

B

A

A

A

Concept - Letter A Revision

Date:_________

Match The Letter With The Images Beginning With The Letter Sound.

A

Let's Learn Letter A

Date:________

Color letter A

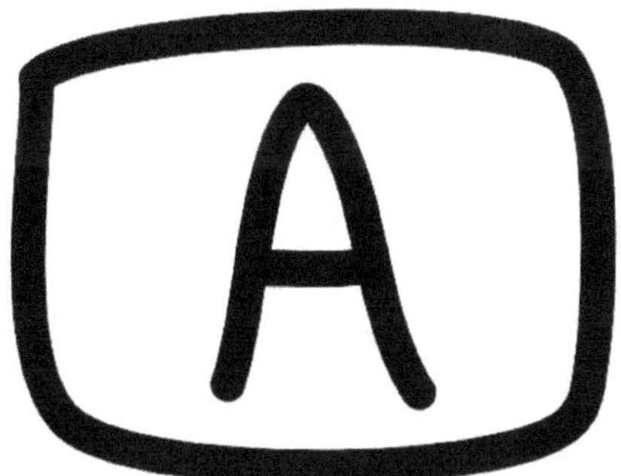

Color the Apple

Find and circle the letter A

A B A A

A B A

Find and color the image starting from letter A

Concept - Letter B

Find And Color Letter B

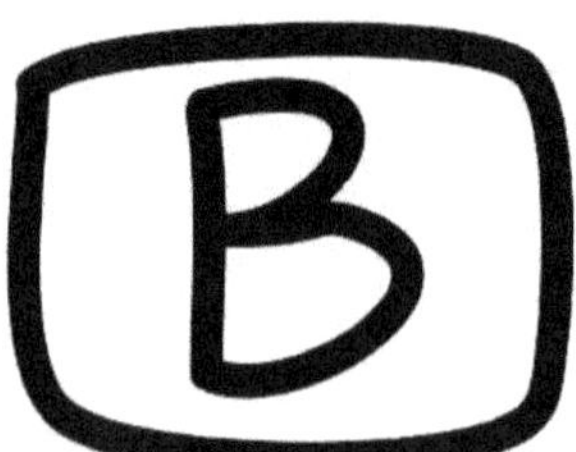

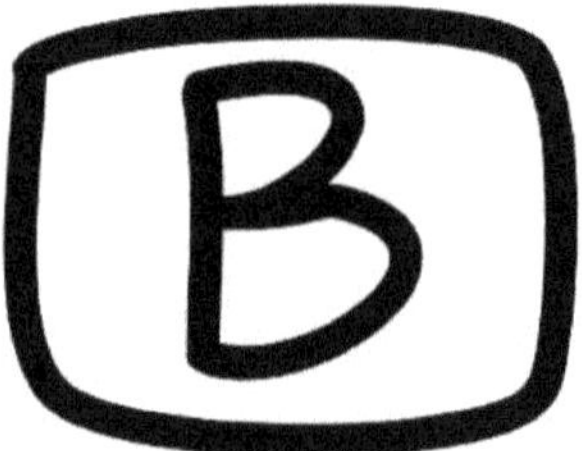

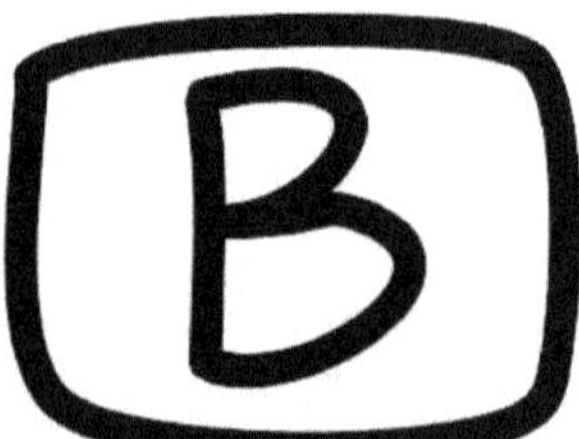

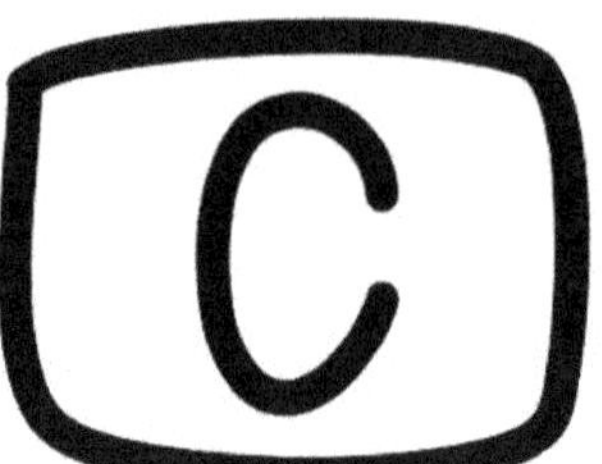

4

Concept - Letters Revision

Date:__________

Match The Letters With The Images Beginning With The Letter Sound.

A

B

Let's Learn Letter B   Date:________

Color letter B

Color the Ball

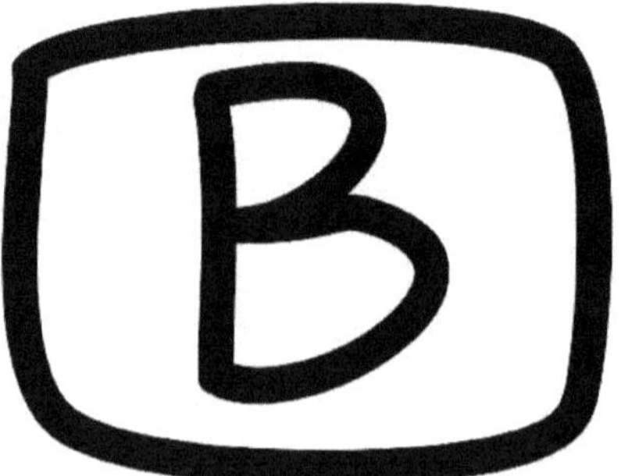

Find and circle the letter B

B

A

A

B

B

A

B

Find and color the images starting from letter B

6

Concept - Letter C

Find And Color Letter C

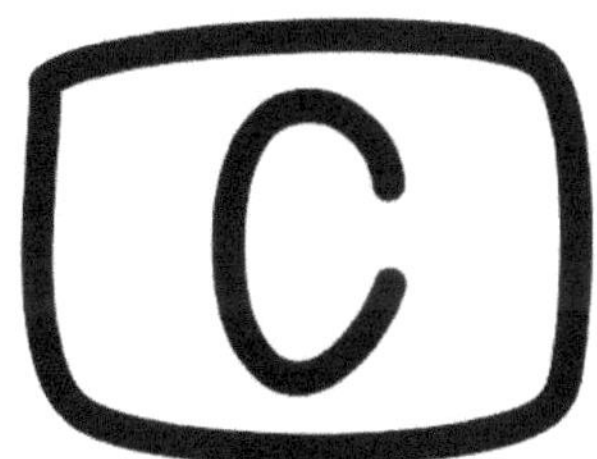

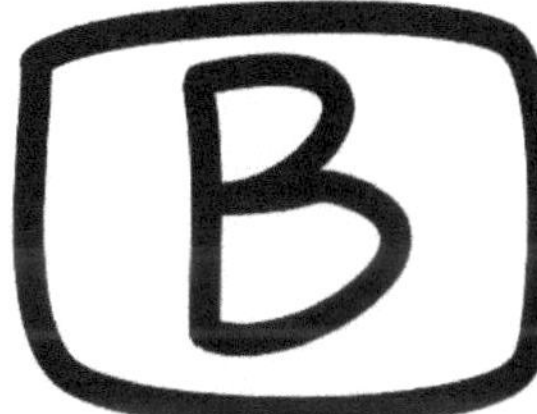
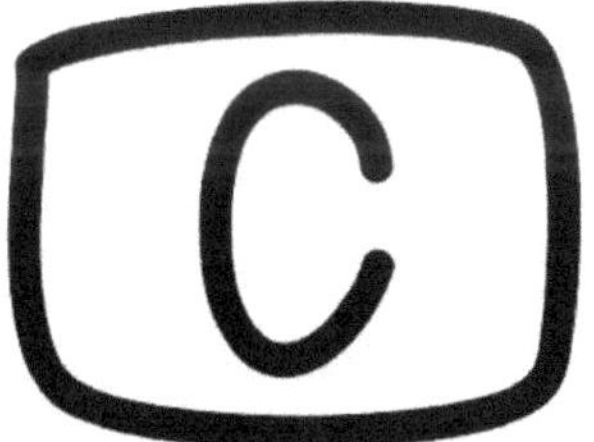
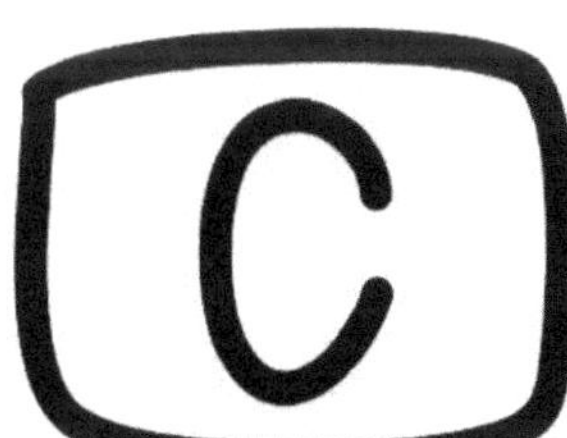
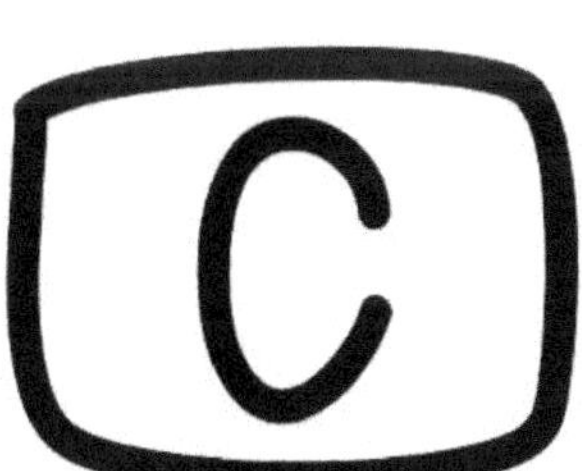
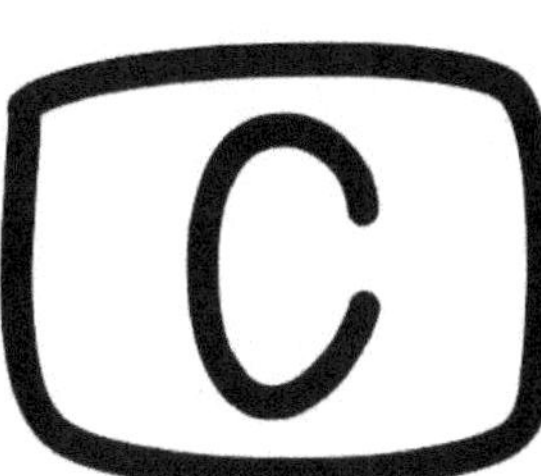

Concept - Letters Revision

Match The Letters With The Images Beginning With The Letter Sound.

A

B

C

Let's Learn Letter C

Date:________

Color letter C

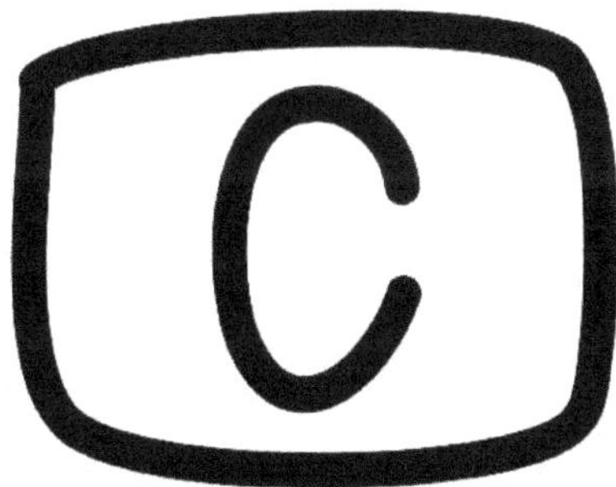

Color the Car

Find and circle the letter C

C   C   C

B

C   B   C

Find and color the images starting from letter C

9

Concept - Letter D

Find And Color Letter D

Date:_________

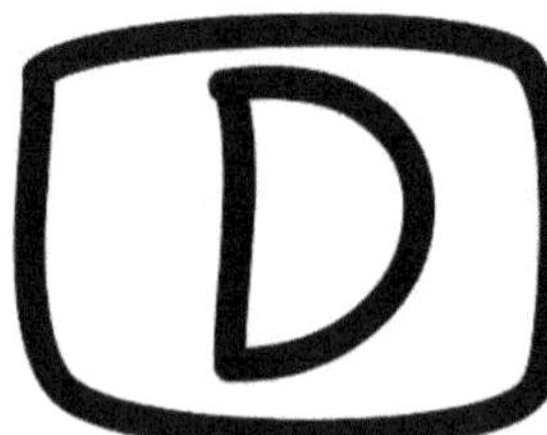
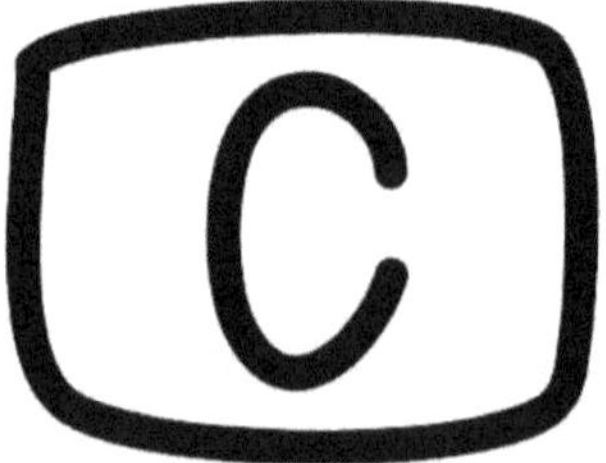
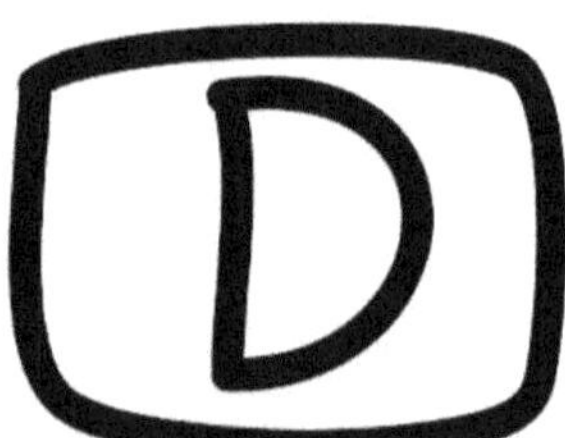
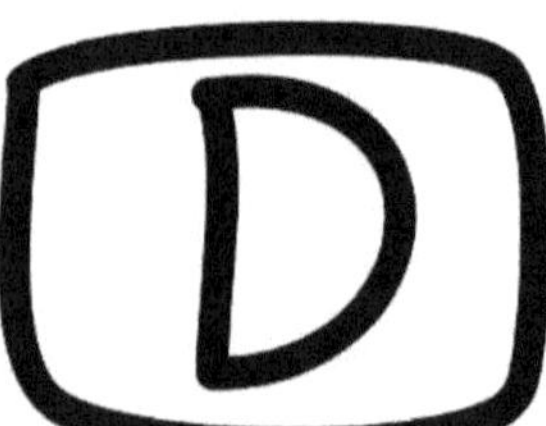
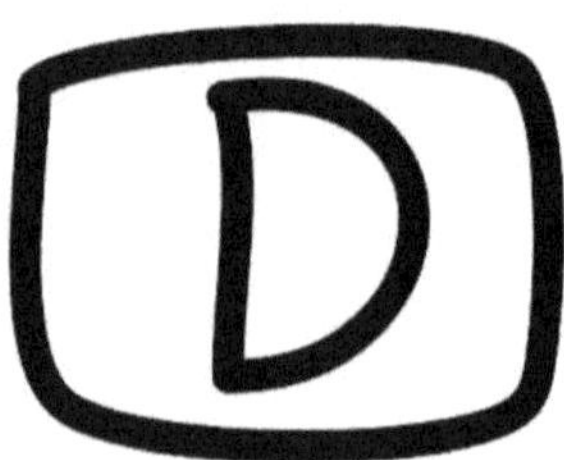
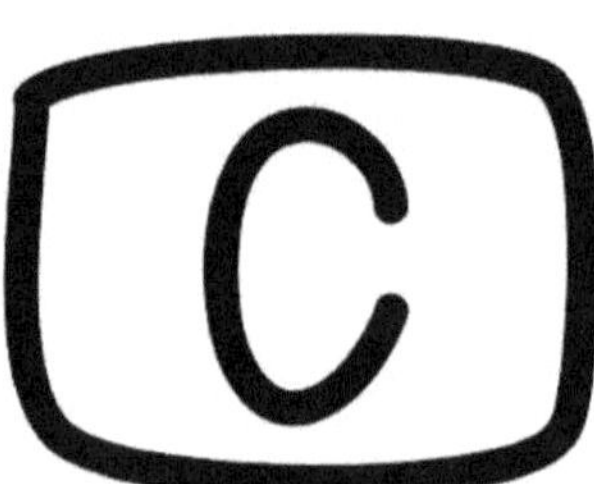

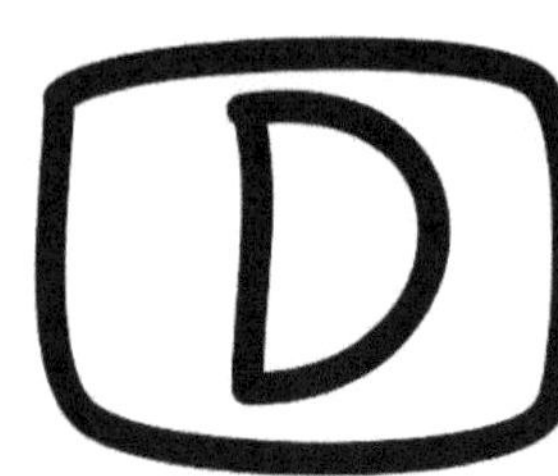

Concept - Letters Revision

Date:__________

Match The Letters With The Images Beginning With The Letter Sound.

B

C

D

Let's Learn Letter D

Color letter D

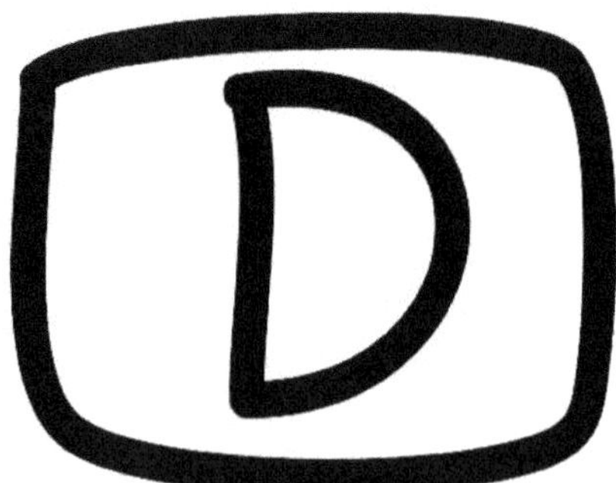

Color the Dolphin

Find and circle the letter D

D C D

C

D D D

Find and color the images starting from letter D

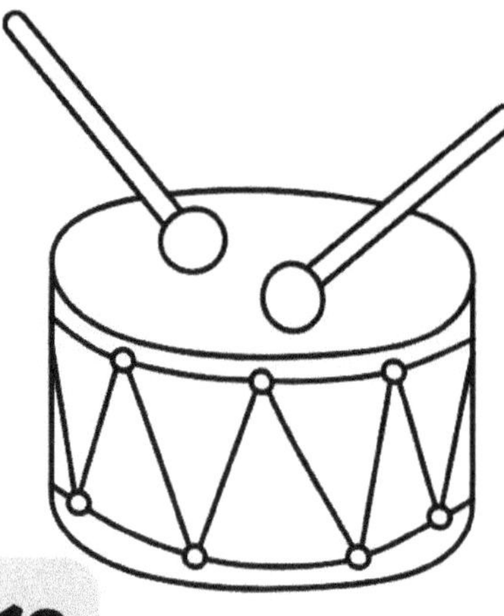

Concept - Letter E

Find And Color Letter E

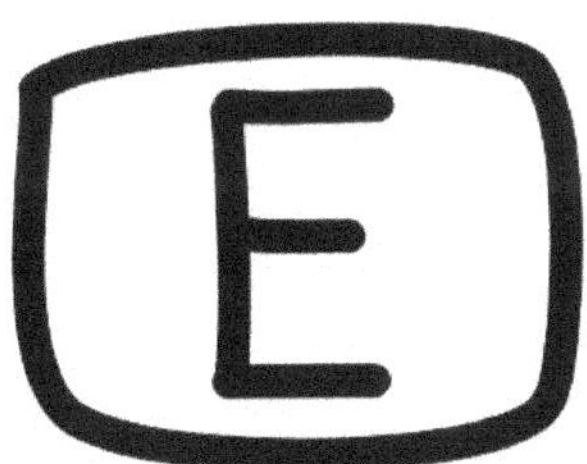

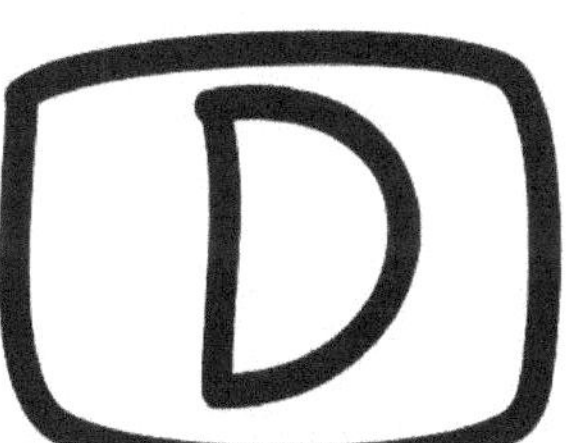

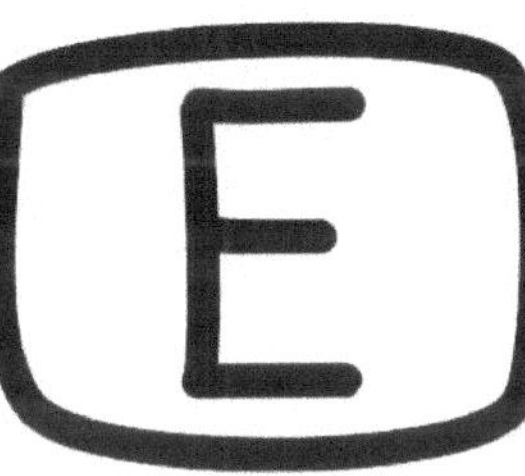

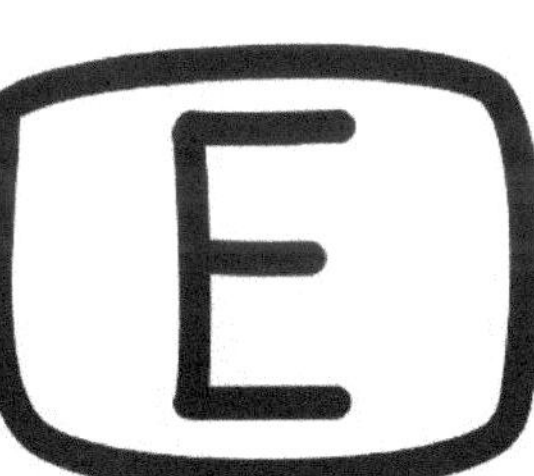

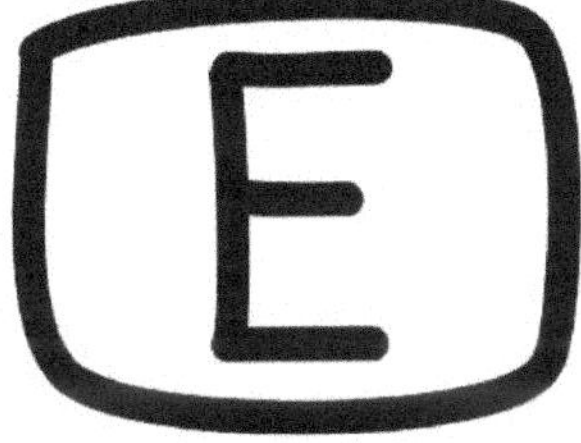

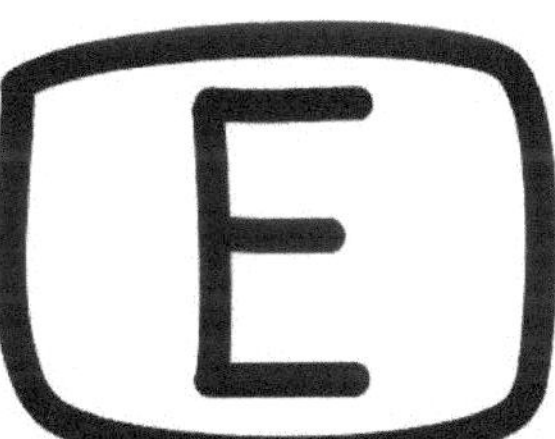

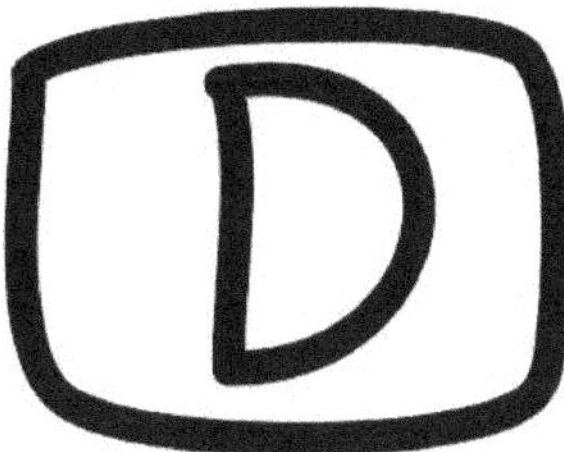

Concept - Letters Revision

Match The Letters With The Images Beginning With The Letter Sound.

C

D

E

Let's Learn Letter E

Color letter E

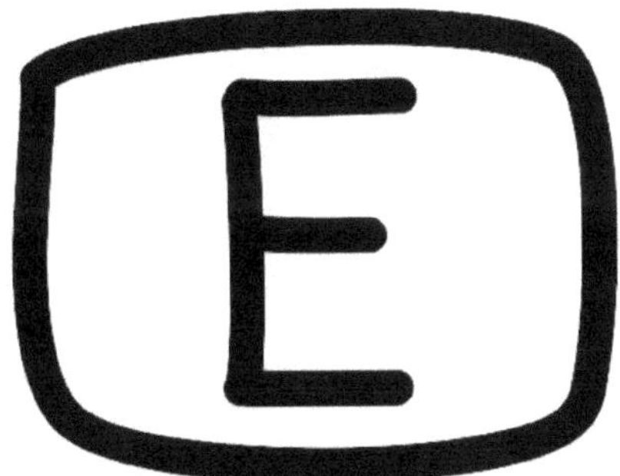

Color the Egg

Find and circle the letter E

D   E   D

E

D   E   E

Find and color the images starting from letter E

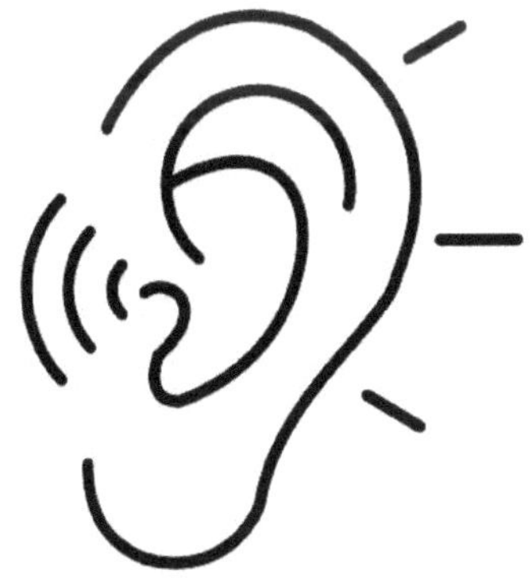

15

Concept - Letter F

Find And Color Letter F

Date:_________

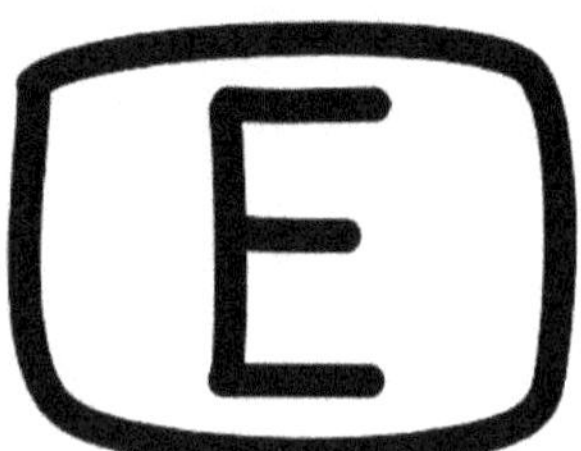

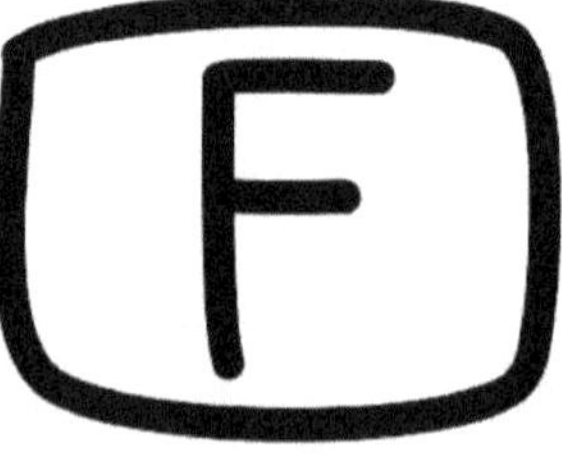

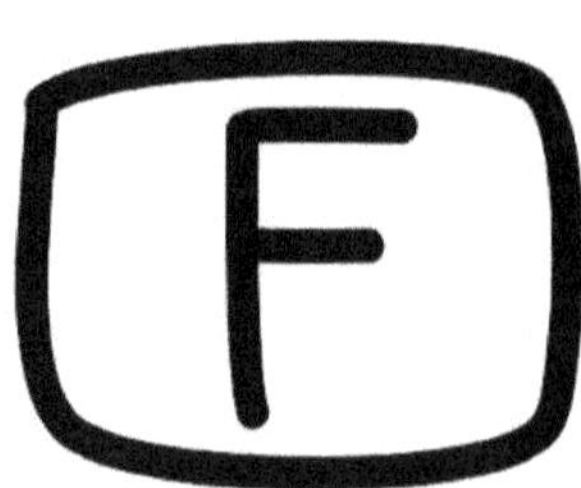

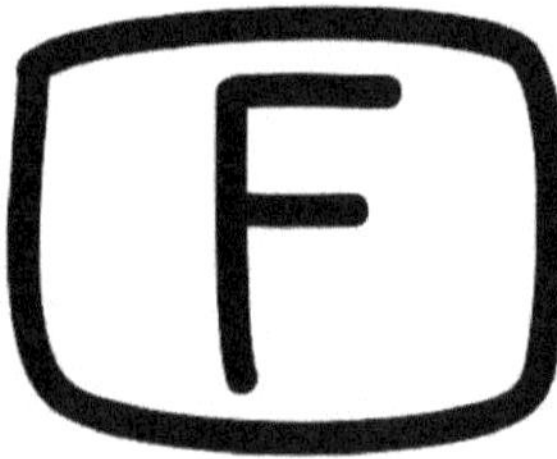

16

Concept - Letters Revision

Date:_________

Match The Letters With The Images Beginning With The Letter Sound.

D

E

F

17

Let's Learn Letter F

Date:________

Color letter F

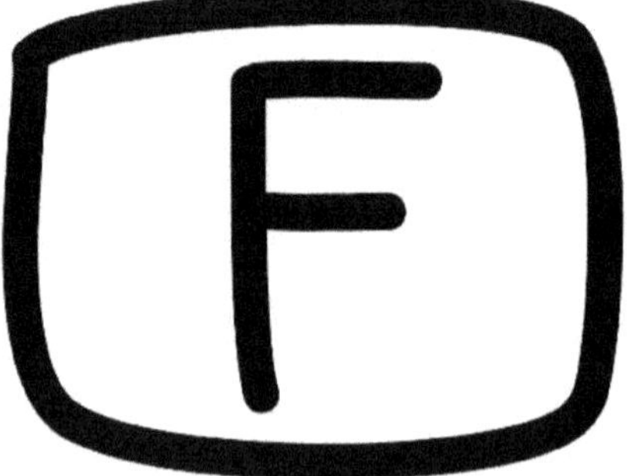

Color the Fish

E   F   F

F

E   F   F

18

Concept - Letter G

Find And Color Letter G

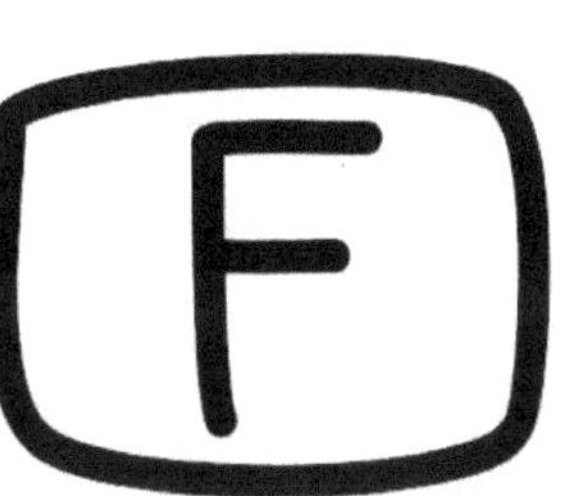

Concept - Letters Revision

Date:__________

Match The Letters With The Images Beginning With The Letter Sound.

E

F

G

Let's Learn Letter G   Date:________

Color letter G

G

Color the Goat

G   F   G

G

F   G   G

Concept - Letter H

Find And Color Letter H

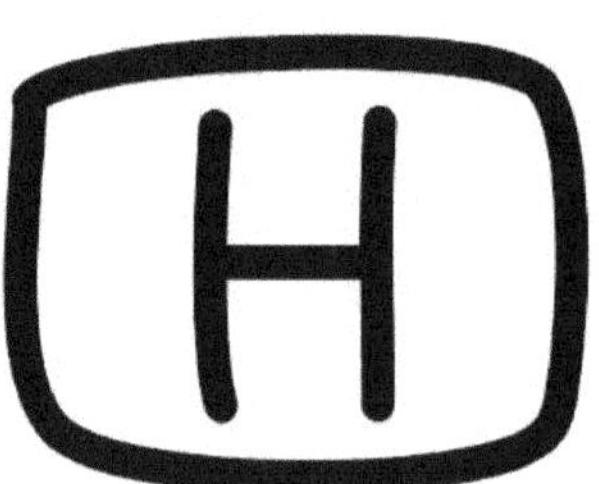

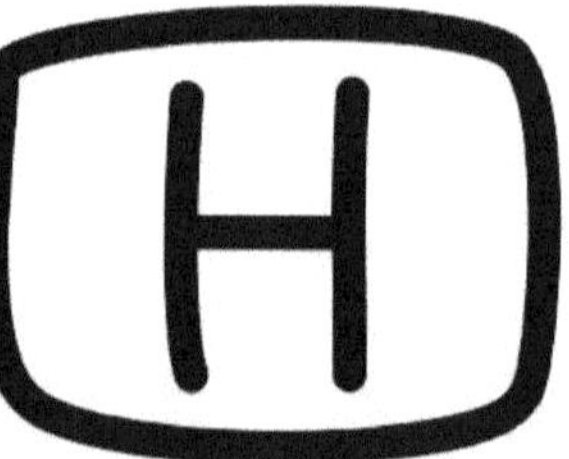
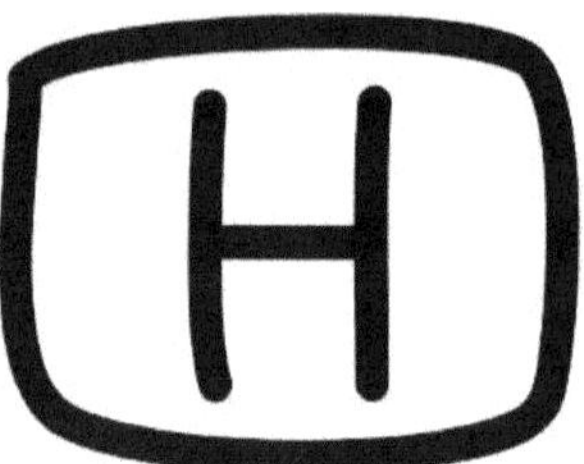

22

Concept - Letters Revision

Match The Letters With The Images Beginning With The Letter Sound.

F

G

H

23

Let's Learn Letter H

Date:________

Color letter H

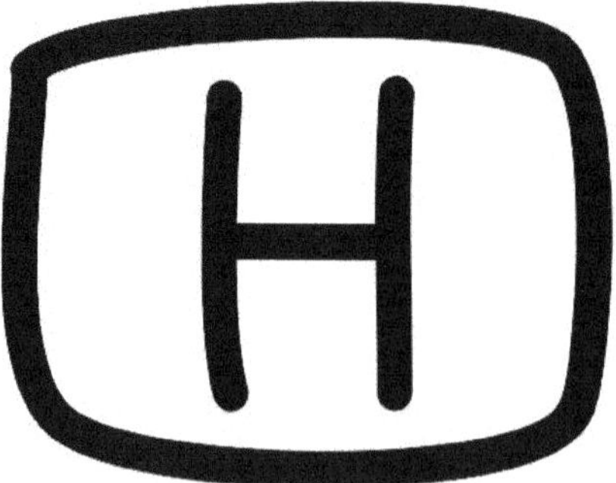

Color the Horse

Find and circle the letter H

H G G H

H G H H

Find and color the images starting from letter H

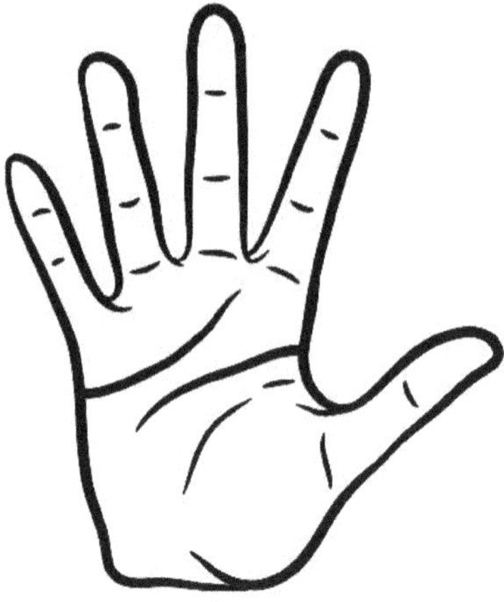

24

Find And Color Letter I

Date:_________

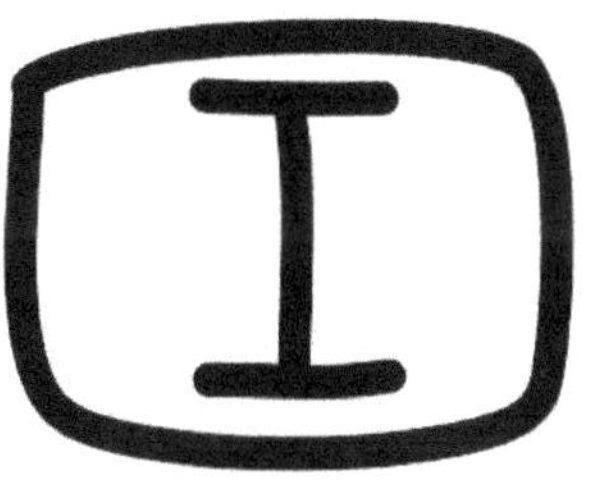
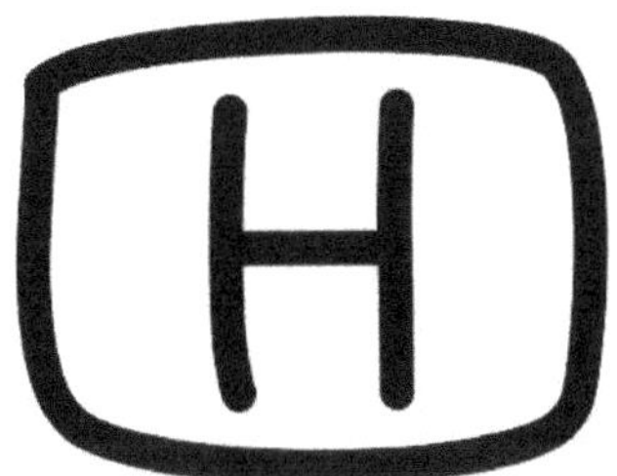
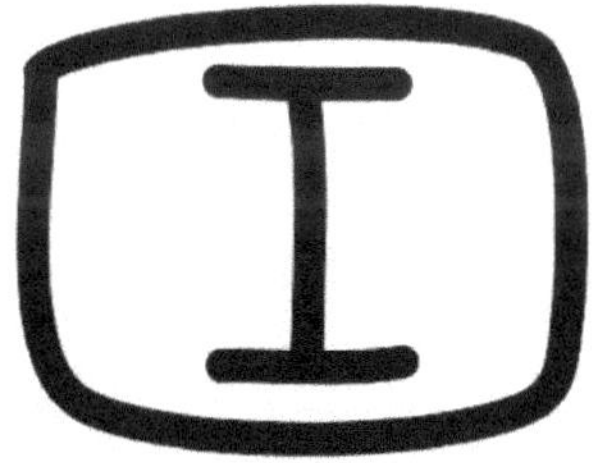
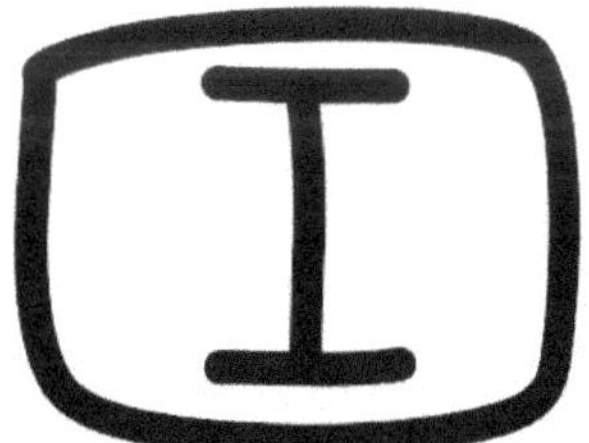

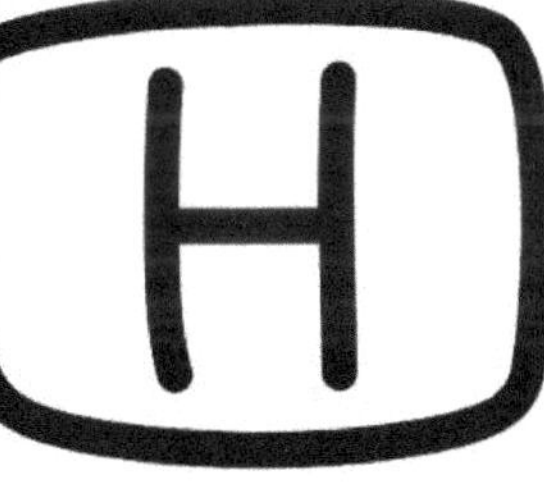

Concept - Letters Revision

Match The Letters With The Images Beginning With The Letter Sound.

G

H

I

26

Let's Learn Letter I

Date:________

Color letter I

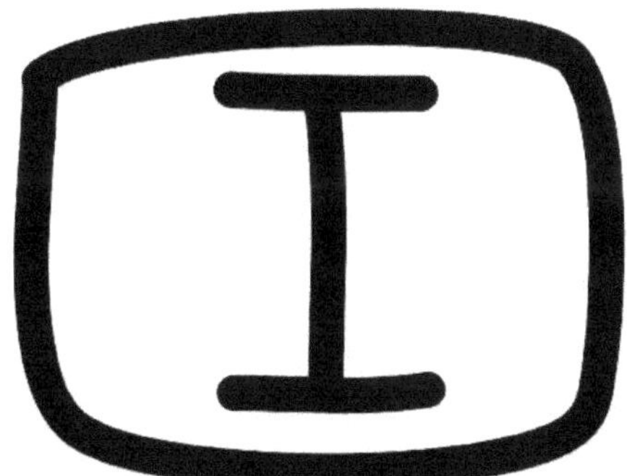

Color the Igloo

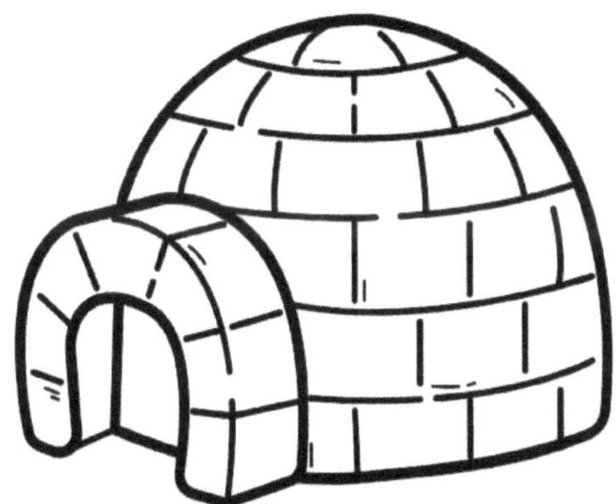

H   H   I

   I   I

I   I   H

Concept - Letter J

Find And Color Letter J

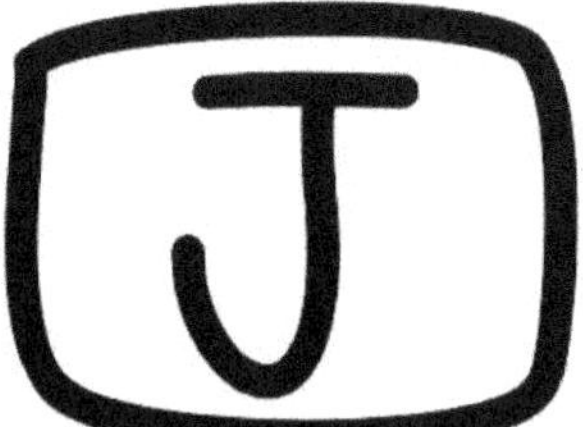

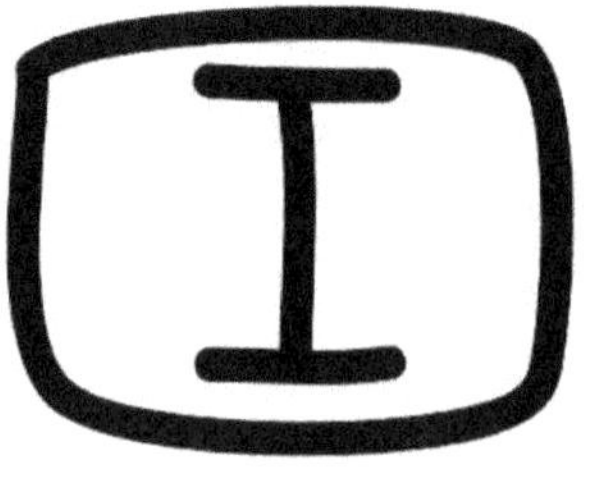

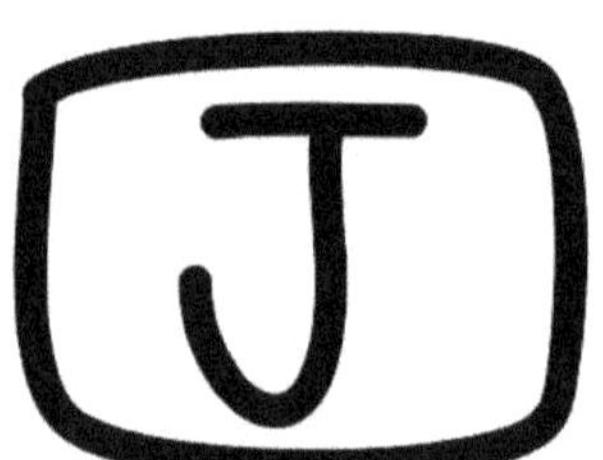

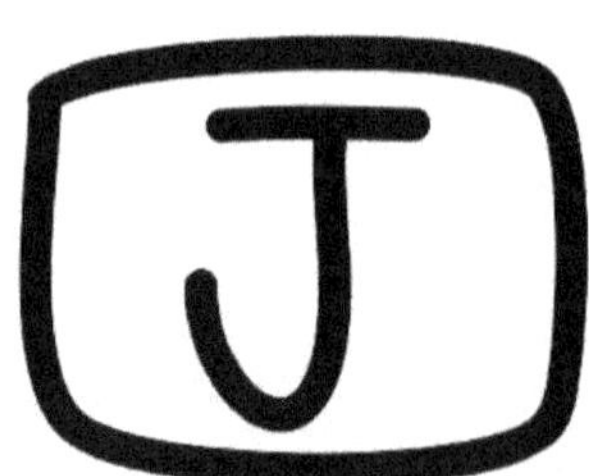

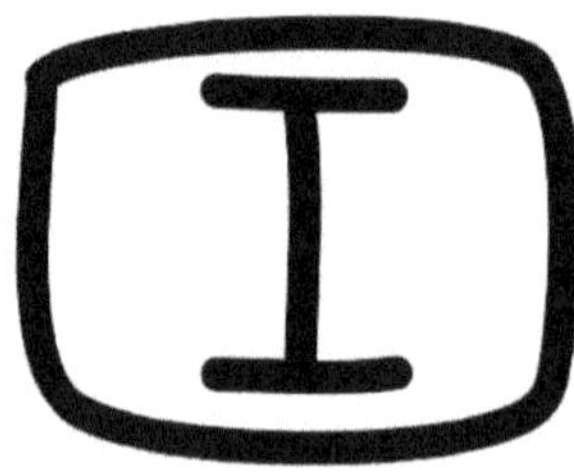

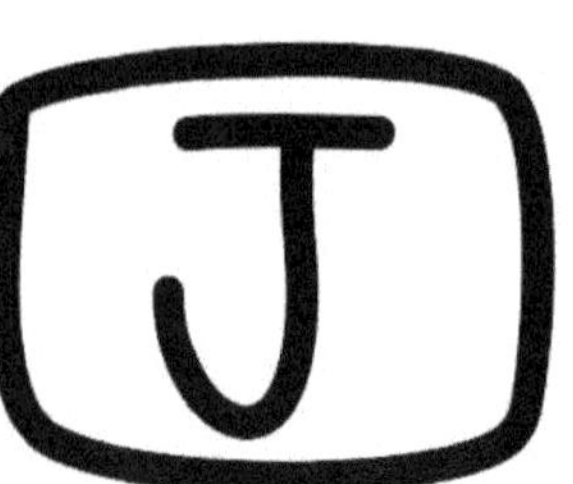

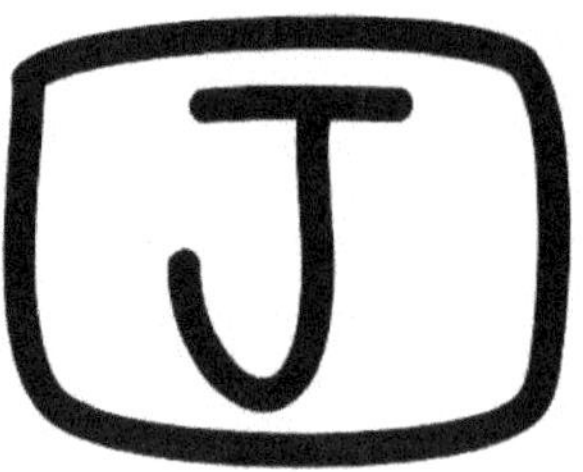

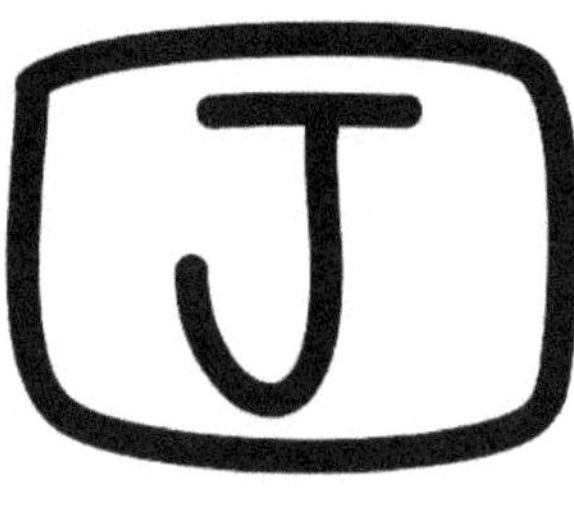

28

Concept - Letters Revision

Date:__________

Match The Letters With The Images Beginning With The Letter Sound.

H

I

J

Let's Learn Letter J

Date:_________

Color letter J

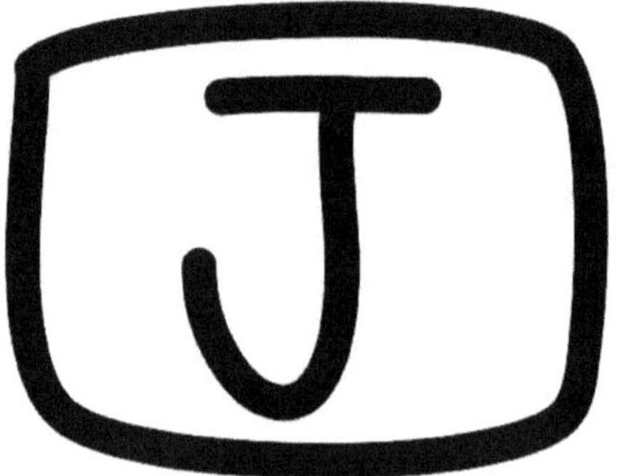

Color the Jug

Find and circle the letter J

I J J

J

J

J I A

Find and color the images starting from letter J

30

Concept - Letter K

Date:_________

Find And Color Letter K

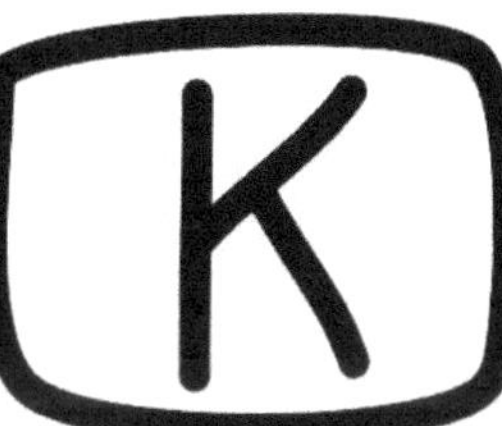

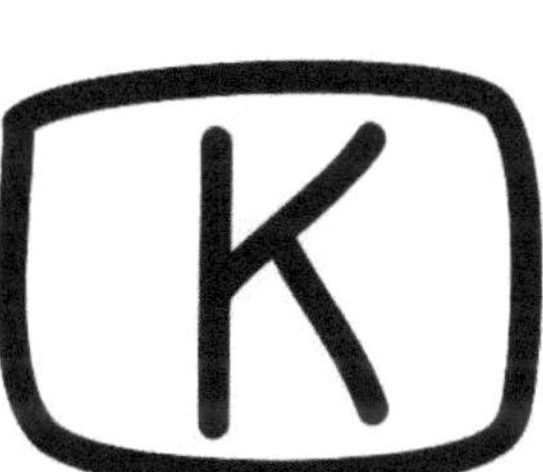
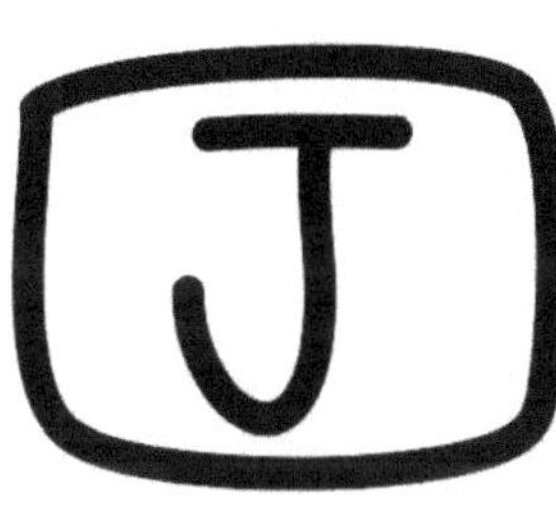

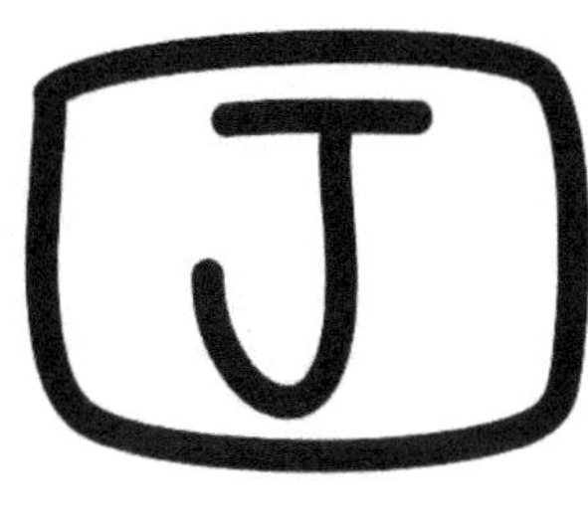

Concept - Letters Revision

Date:__________

Match The Letters With The Images Beginning With The Letter Sound.

I

J

K

Let's Learn Letter K

Color letter K

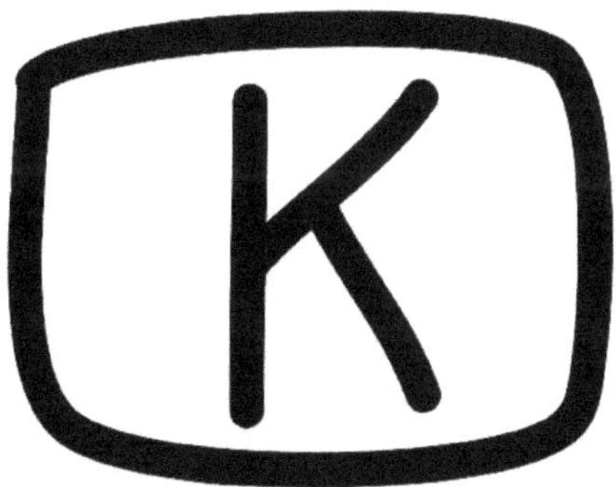

Color the Kite

Find and circle the letter K

K   K   K

J

J   K   K

Find and color the images starting from letter K

Concept - Letter L

Find And Color Letter L

Date:________

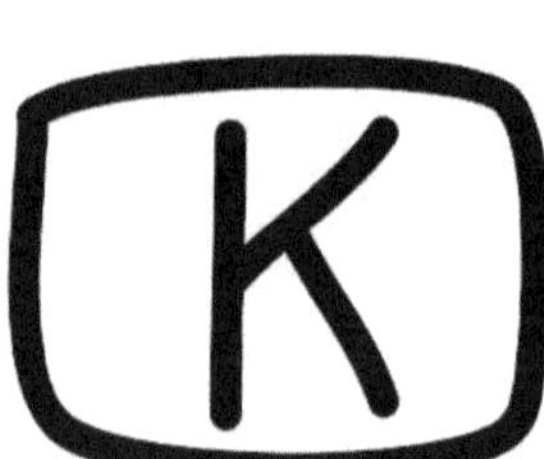

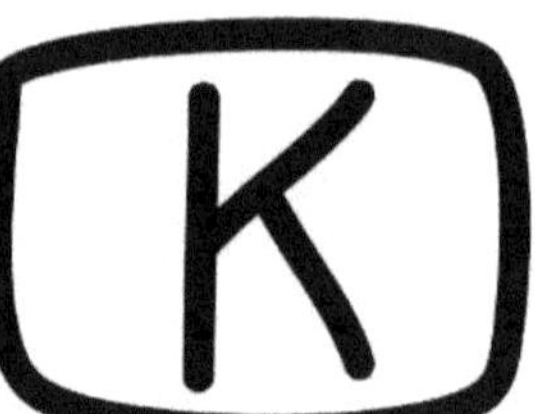

Concept - Letters Revision

Match The Letters With The Images Beginning With The Letter Sound.

J

K

L

35

Let's Learn Letter L

Date:________

Color letter L

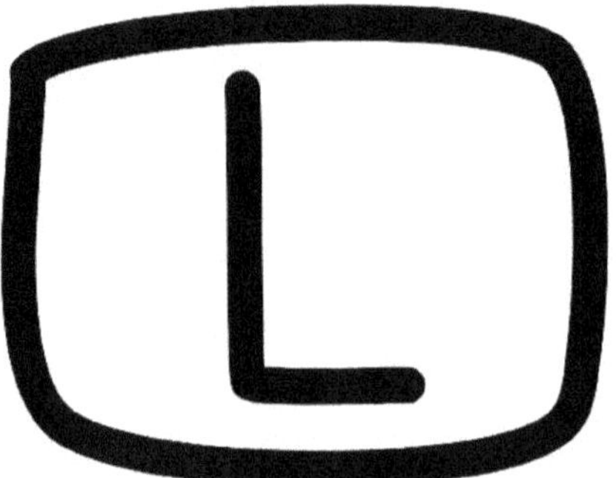

Color the Lamp

Find and circle the letter L

K L L L
K L L A
L

Find and color the images starting from letter L

36

Concept - Letter M

Find And Color Letter M

Date:__________

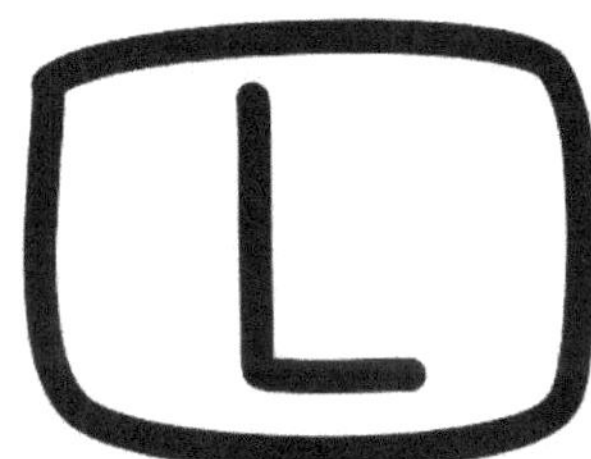

Concept - Letters Revision

Match The Letters With The Images Beginning With The Letter Sound.

K

L

M

Color letter M

Color the Mat

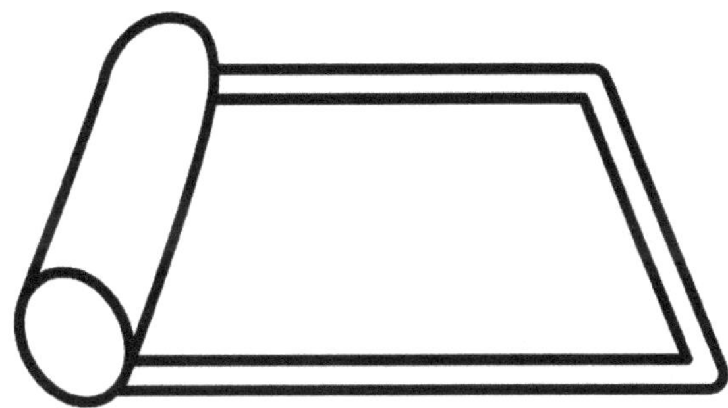

Find and circle the letter M

L M M

M

L M L

Find and color the images starting from letter M

39

Revision Of Letters Till M

Circle The Objects That Begins With That Sound In Each Row

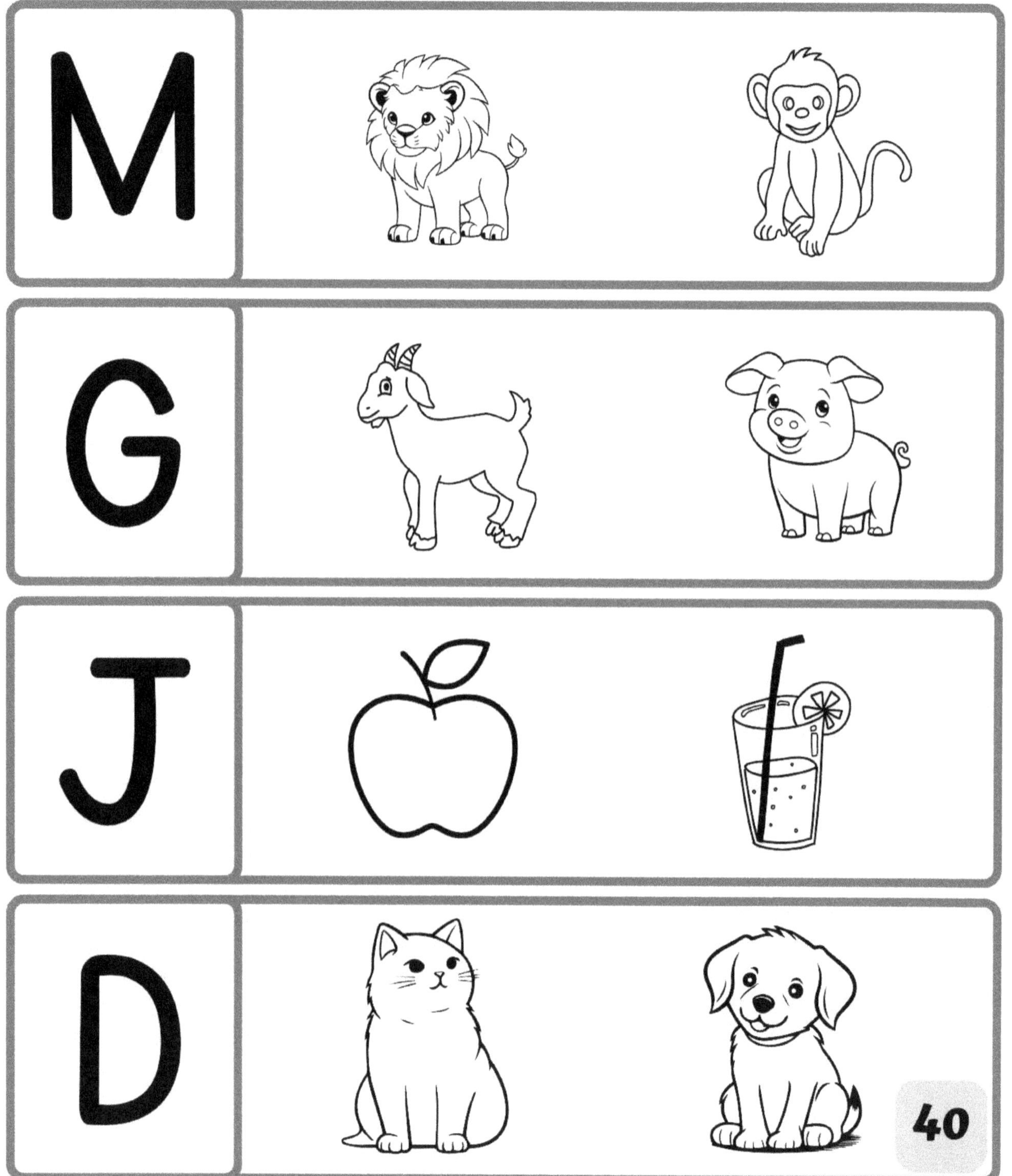

40

Revision Of Letters Till M

Circle The Objects That Begins With That Sound In Each Row

Revision Of Letters Till M

Circle The Objects That Begins With That Sound In Each Row

Concept - Letter N

Find And Color Letter N

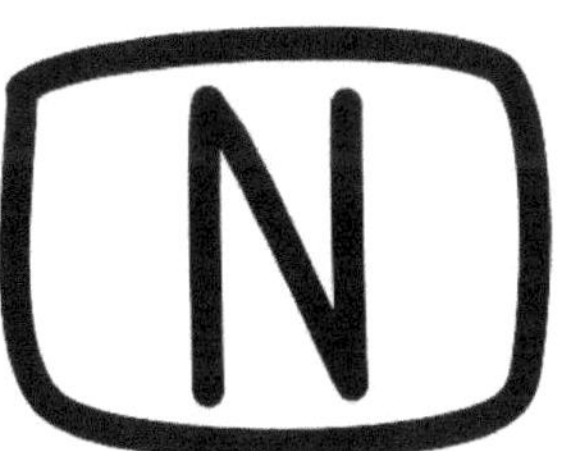

Concept - Letters Revision

Match The Letters With The Images Beginning With The Letter Sound.

K

L

M

N

44

Let's Learn Letter N
Date:________

Color letter N

Color the Nest

Find and circle the letter N

M   N   N

N

M   N   M

Find and color the images starting from letter N

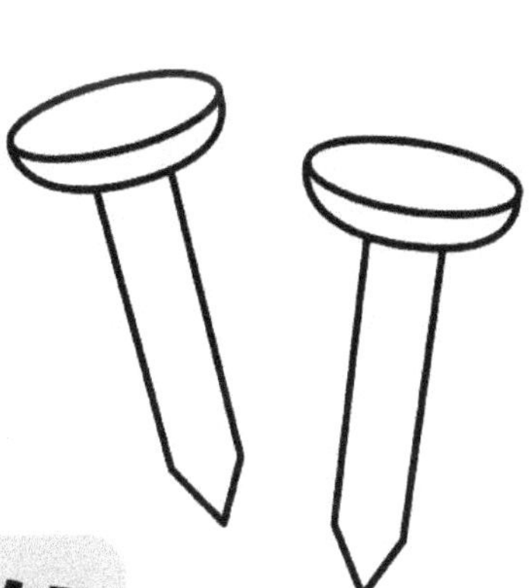

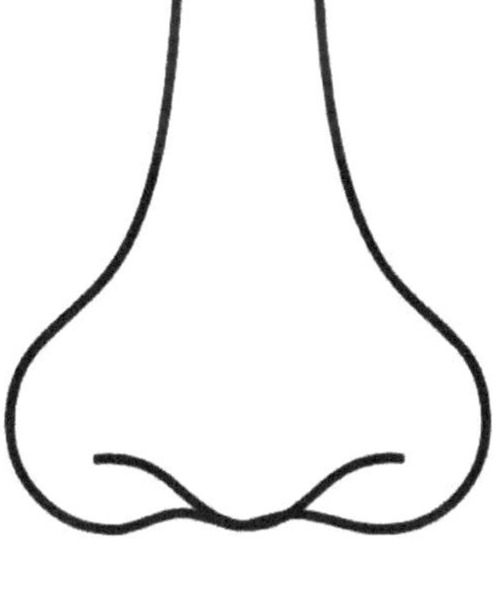

45

Concept - Letter O

Find And Color Letter O

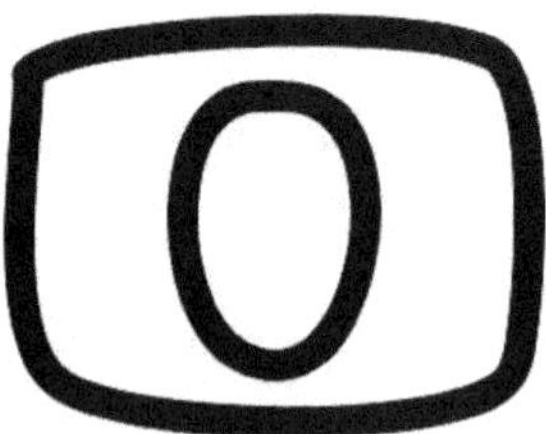

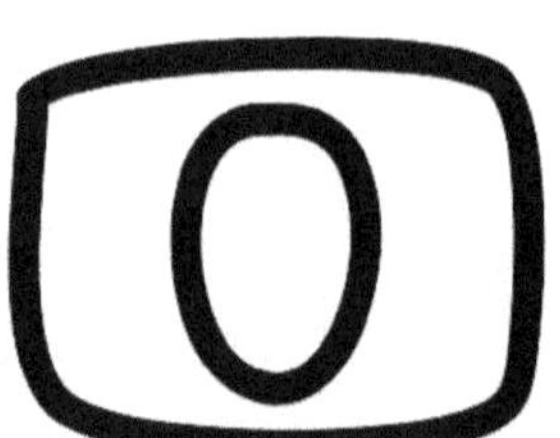

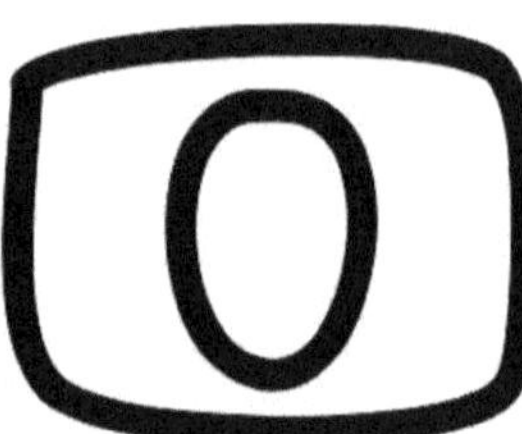

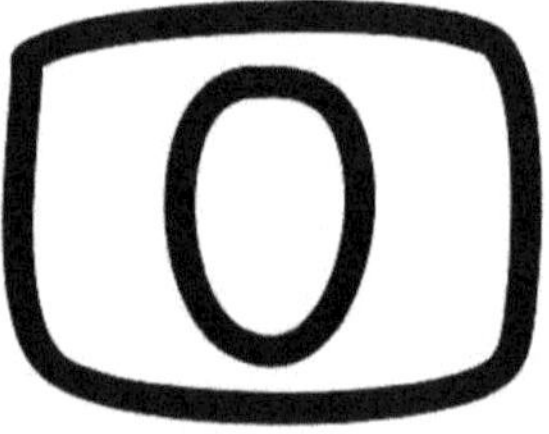

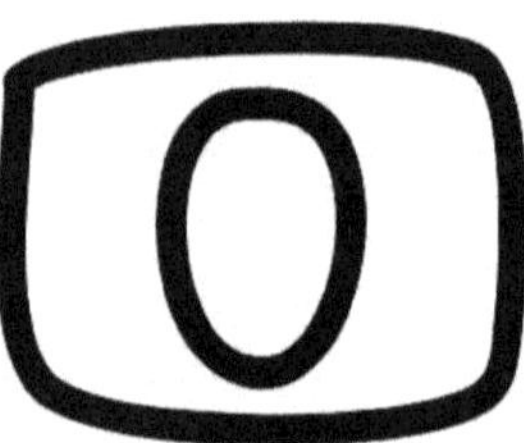

46

Concept - Letters Revision

Match The Letters With The Images Beginning With The Letter Sound.

L

M

N

O

47

Let's Learn Letter O Date:________

Color letter O

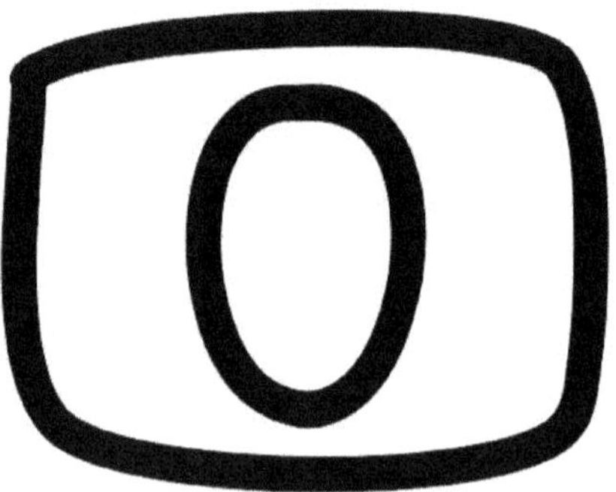

Color the Orange

Find and circle the letter O

N   O   O

O   O

O   N   O

Find and color the images starting from letter O

48

Concept - Letter P

Find And Color Letter P

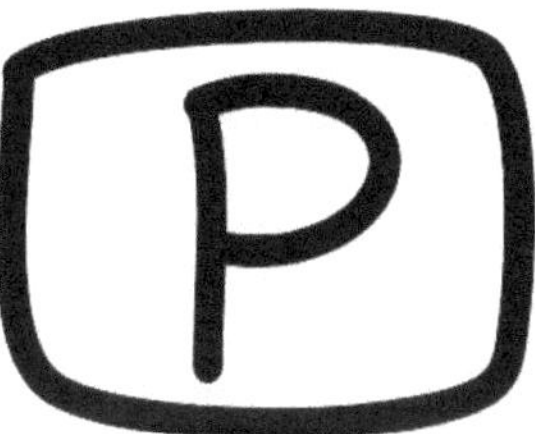

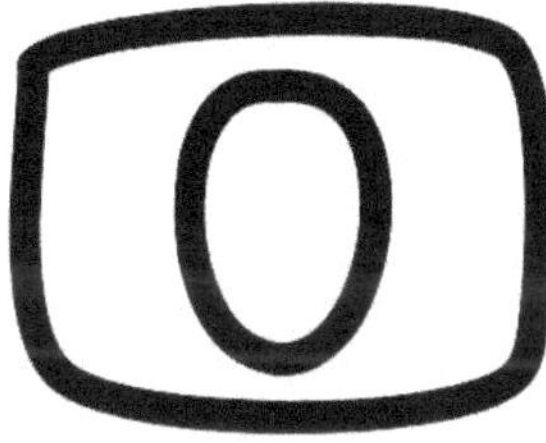

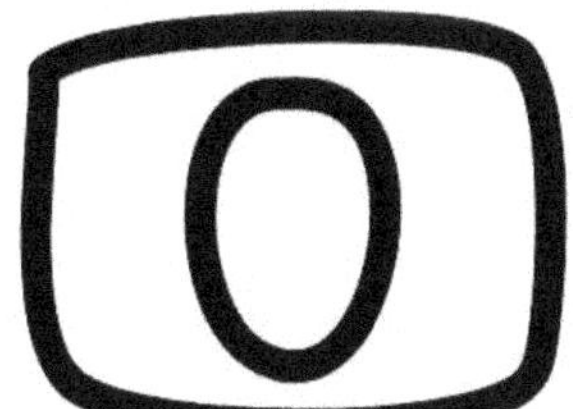

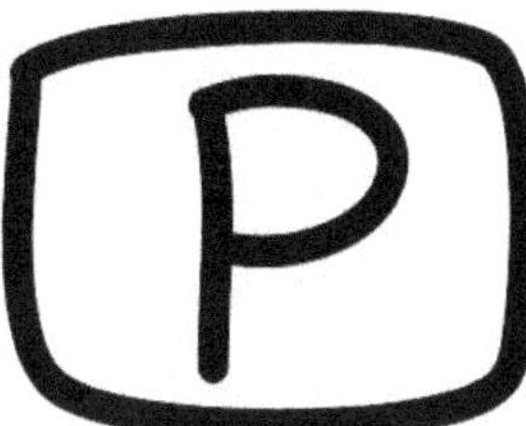

Concept - Letters Revision

Match The Letters With The Images Beginning With The Letter Sound.

M

N

O

P

Let's Learn Letter P Date:_________

Color letter P

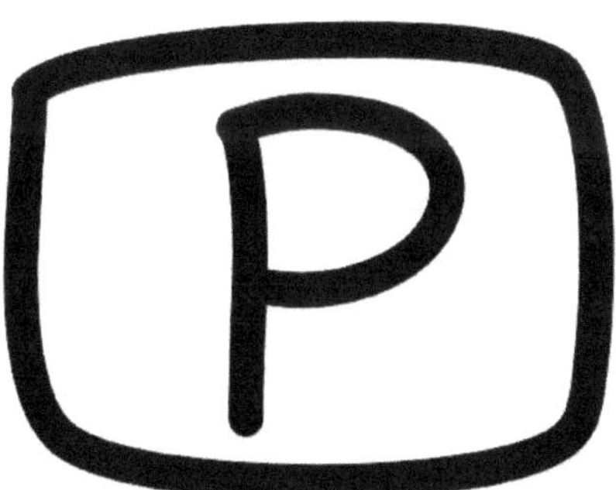

Color the Pumpkin

O

O

P

P

P

P

P

O

51

Concept - Letter Q

Find And Color Letter Q

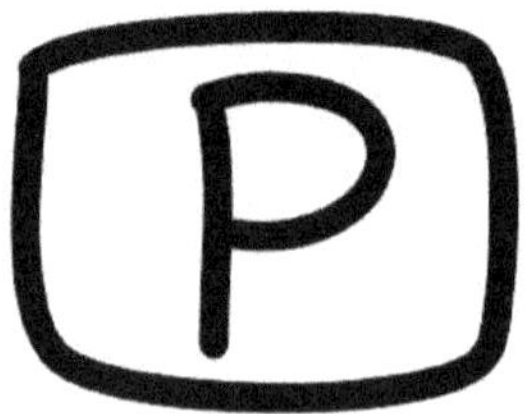

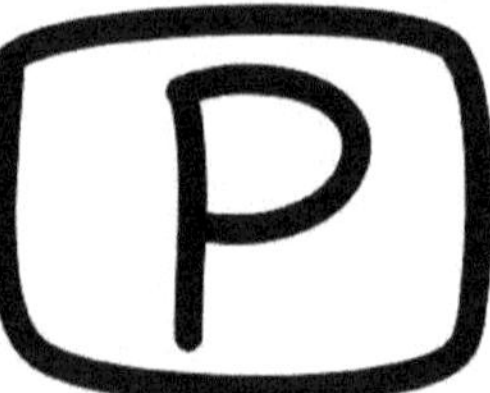

Concept - Letters Revision

Match The Letters With The Images Beginning With The Letter Sound.

N

O

P

Q

Let's Learn Letter Q

Date:________

Color letter Q

Color the Quail

Find and circle the letter Q

P   P   Q

Q

Q   P Q   Q

Find and color the images starting from letter Q

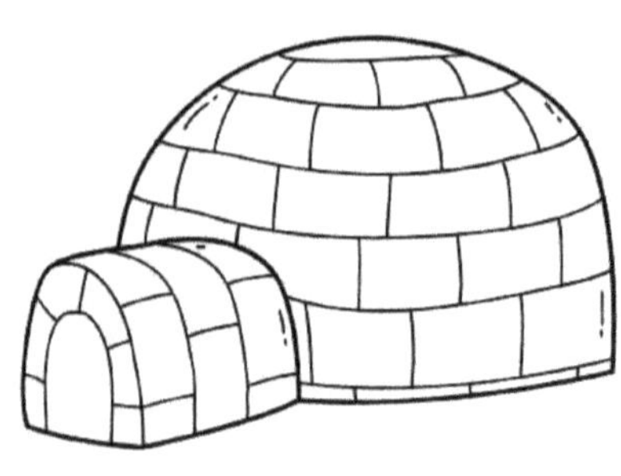

54

Concept - Letter R

Find And Color Letter R

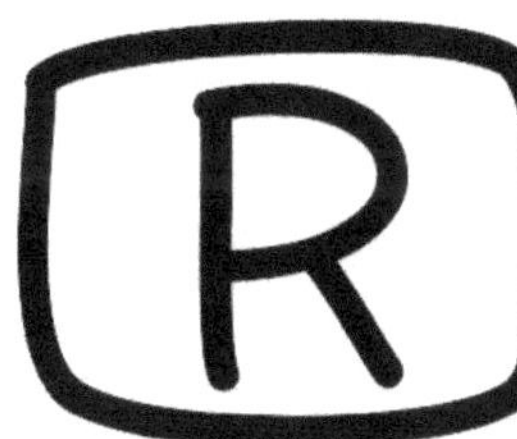

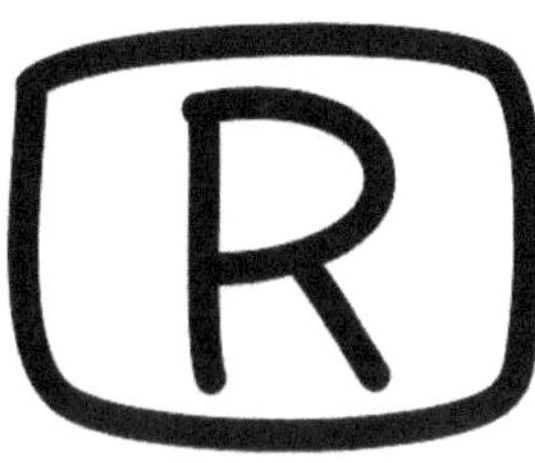
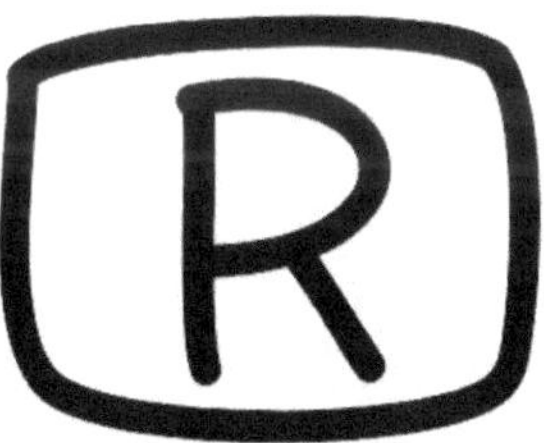
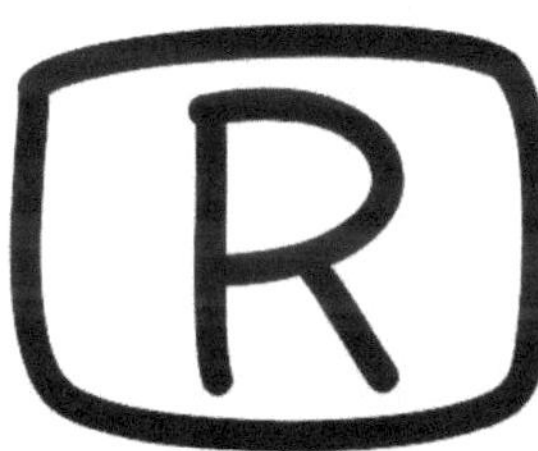

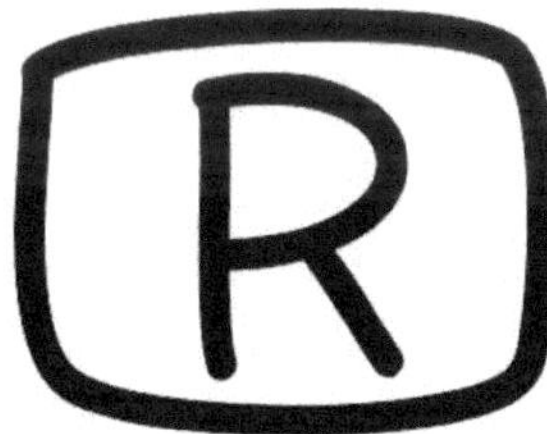

55

Concept - Letters Revision

Match The Letters With The Images Beginning With The Letter Sound.

O

P

Q

R

Let's Learn Letter R Date:________

Color letter R

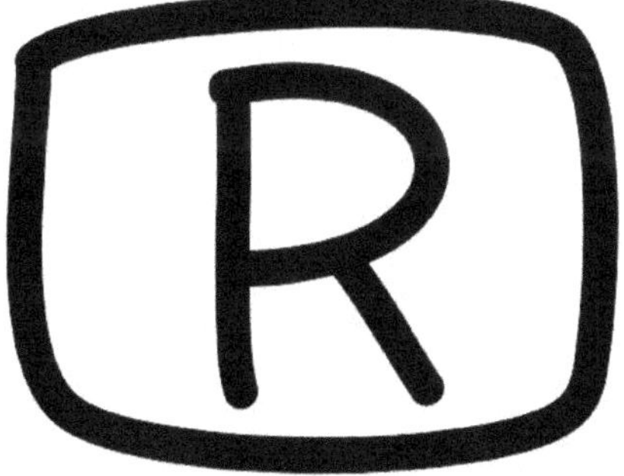

Color the Rocket

Find and circle the letter R

R
R Q R
Q
R R

Find and color the images starting from letter R

Date:_________

Find And Color Letter S

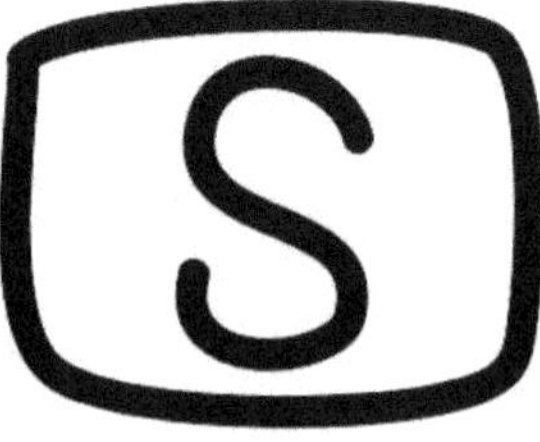

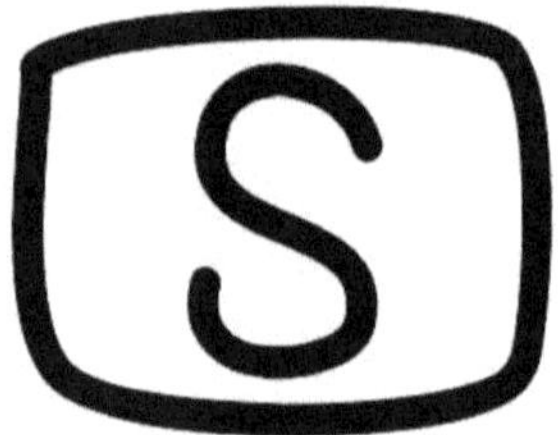

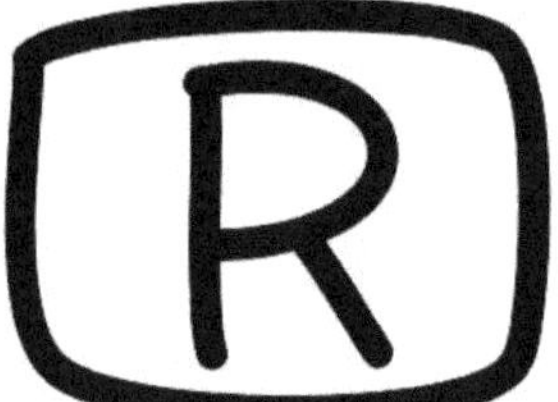

Concept - Letters Revision

Match The Letters With The Images Beginning With The Letter Sound.

P

Q

R

S

Let's Learn Letter S  Date:________

Color letter S

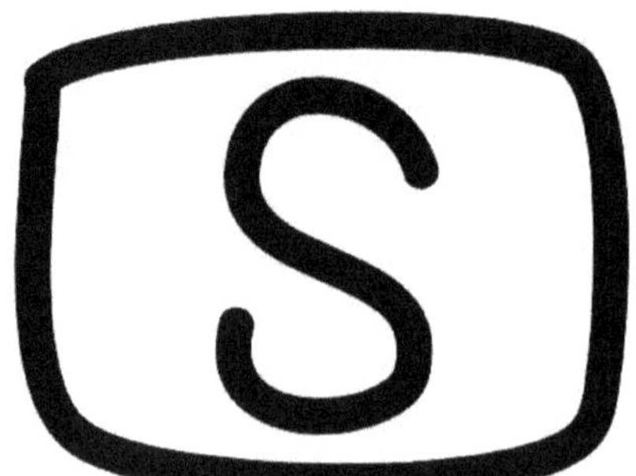

Color the Sock

Find and circle the letter S

S   S   S

S   S

R   R   S

Find and color the images starting from letter S

Concept - Letter T

Find And Color Letter T

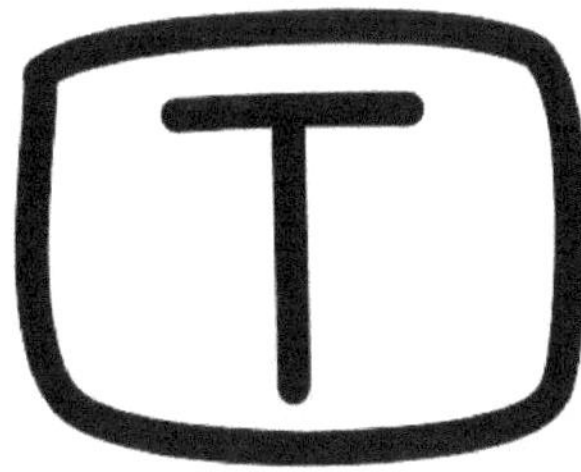
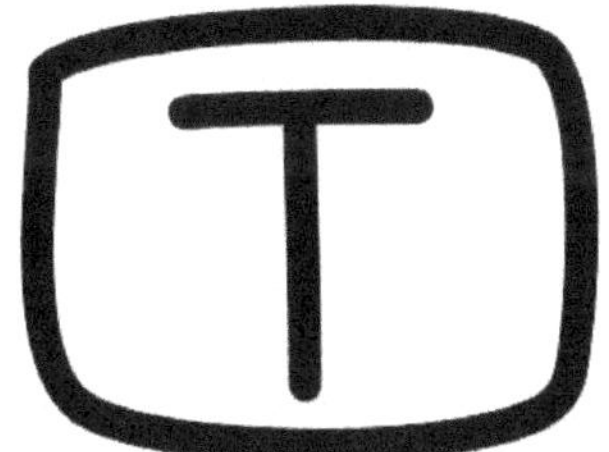

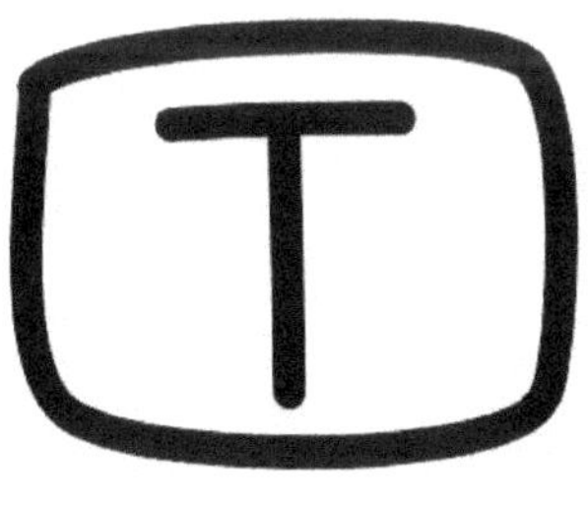

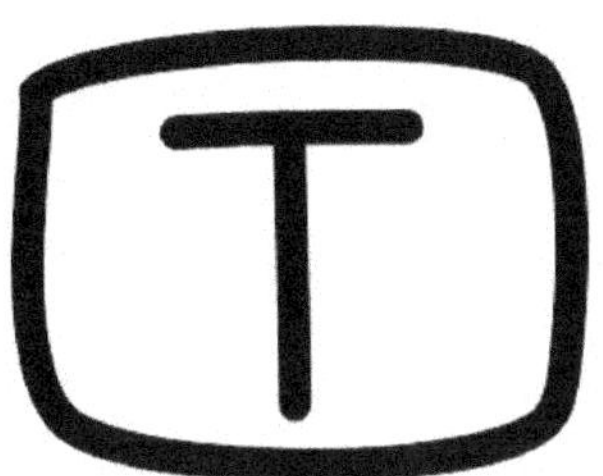
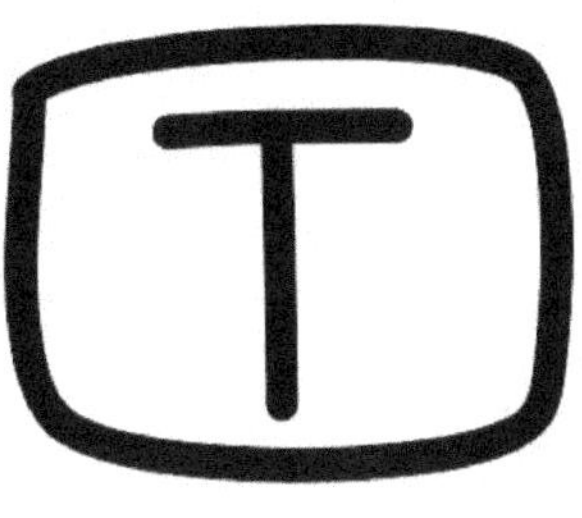

61

Concept - Letters Revision

Match The Letters With The Images Beginning With The Letter Sound.

Q

R

S

T

Let's Learn Letter T

Date:_________

Color letter T

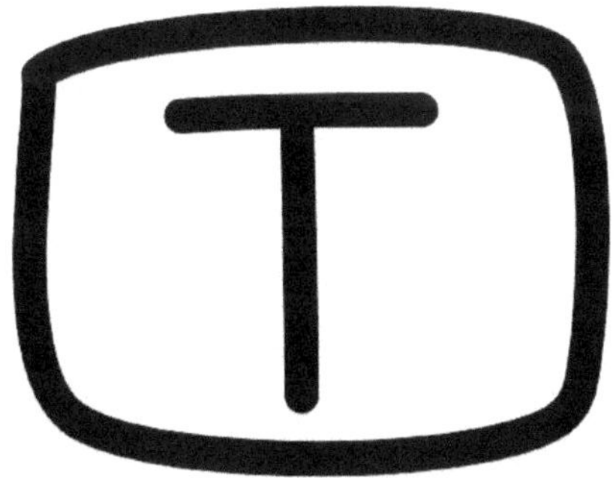

Color the Tree

Find and circle the letter T

T   T   S

T

S   T   T

Find and color the images starting from letter T

Concept - Letter U

Find And Color Letter U

Date:_________

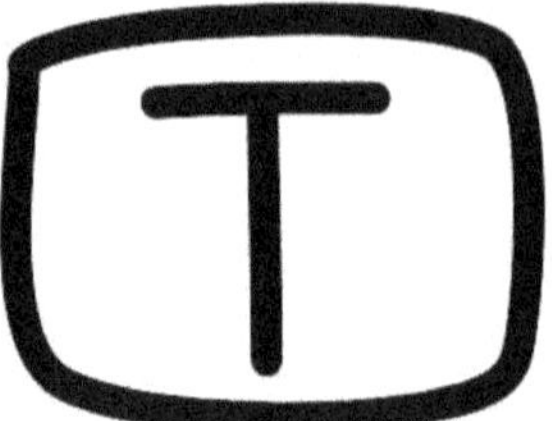

64

Concept - Letters Revision

Date:_________

Match The Letters With The Images Beginning With The Letter Sound.

R

S

T

U

Let's Learn Letter U Date:_________

Color letter U

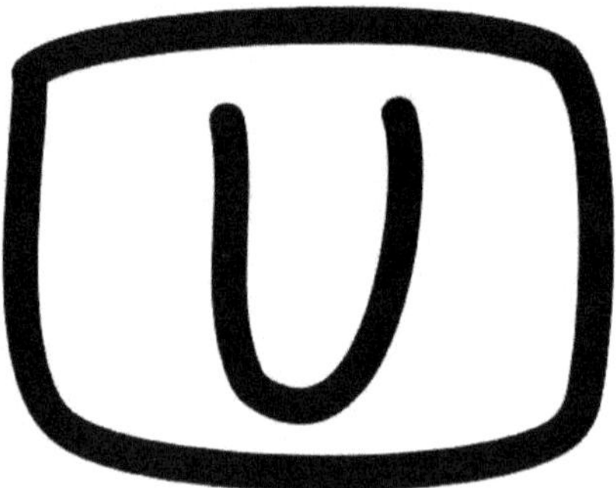

Color the Umbrella

Find and circle the letter U

U
u
T
U
u
T
u
U

Find and color the images starting from letter U

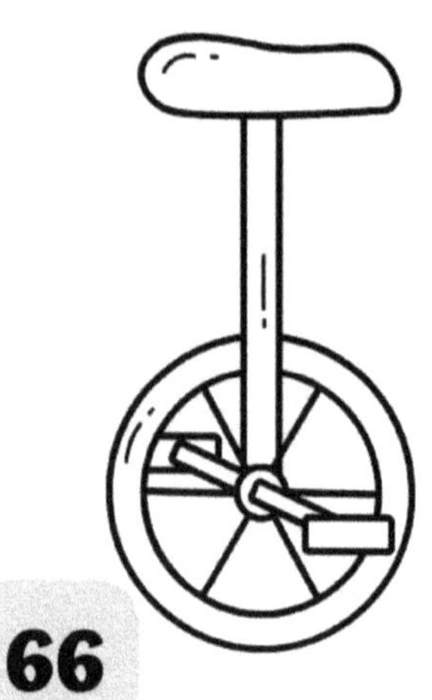

Concept - Letter V

Find And Color Letter V

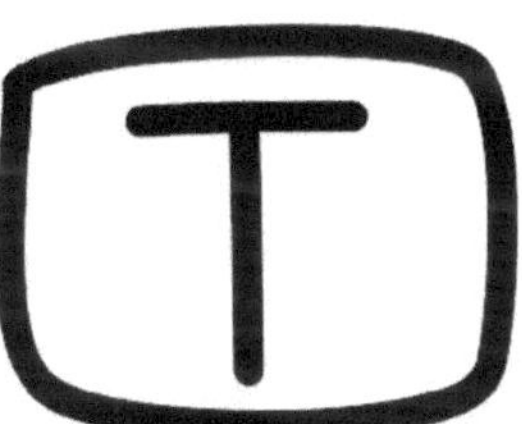

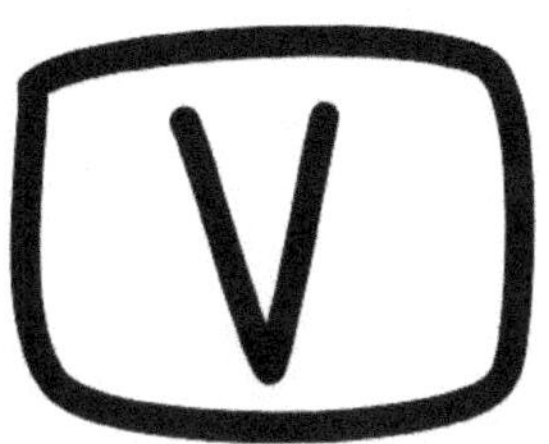

67

Concept - Letters Revision

Match The Letters With The Images Beginning With The Letter Sound.

S

T

U

V

Let's Learn Letter V Date:_________

Color letter V

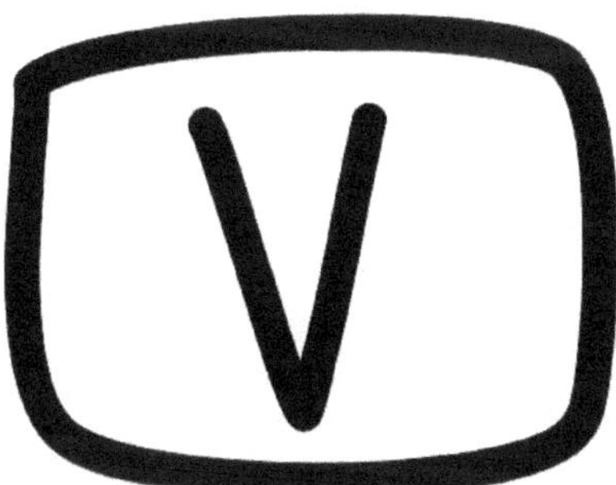

Color the Van

Find and circle the letter V

U   U   V

V   V

V   V

Find and color the images starting from letter V

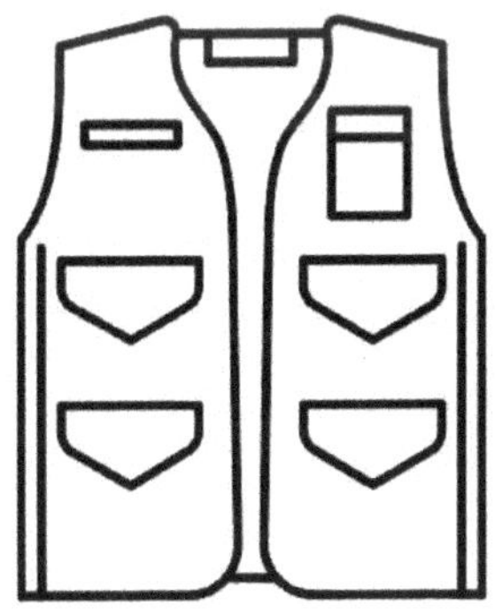

69

Concept - Letter W

Find And Color Letter W

Date:_________

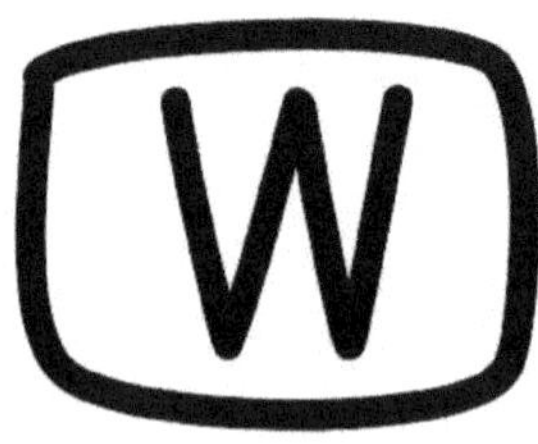

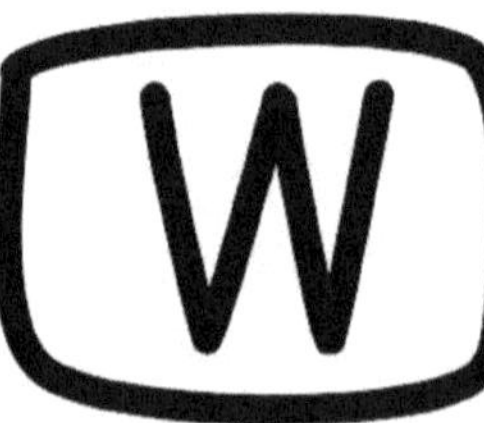

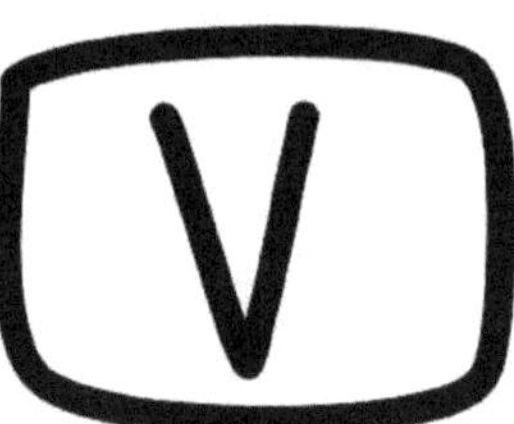

Concept - Letters Revision

Match The Letters With The Images Beginning With The Letter Sound.

T

U

V

W

Let's Learn Letter W Date:________

Color letter W

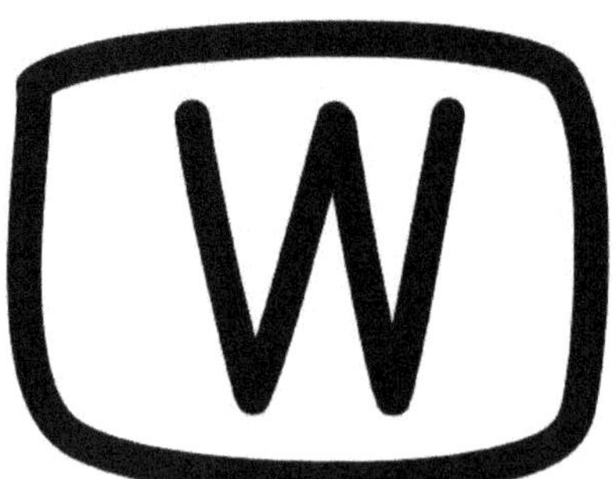

Color the Whale

Find and circle the letter W

V   W

W

W   V

W   W   W

Find and color the images starting from letter W

Concept - Letter X

Find And Color Letter X

Concept - Letters Revision

Date:_________

Match The Letters With The Images Beginning With The Letter Sound.

U

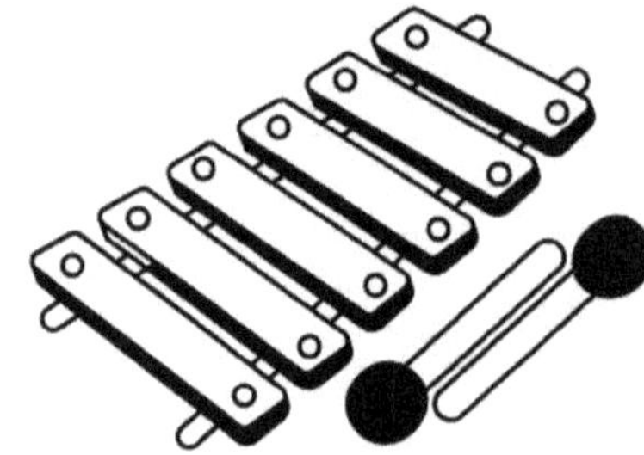

V

W

X

74

Let's Learn Letter X Date:________

Color letter X

Color the Xylophone

Find and circle the letter X

W   X   X

X

X   W   X

Find and color the images starting from letter X

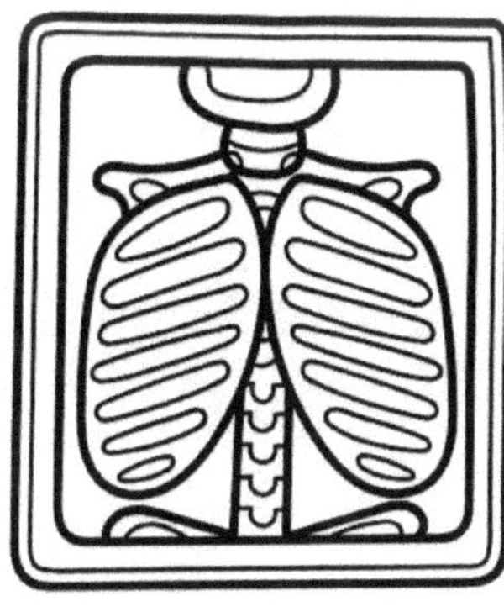

75

Concept - Letter Y

Find And Color Letter Y

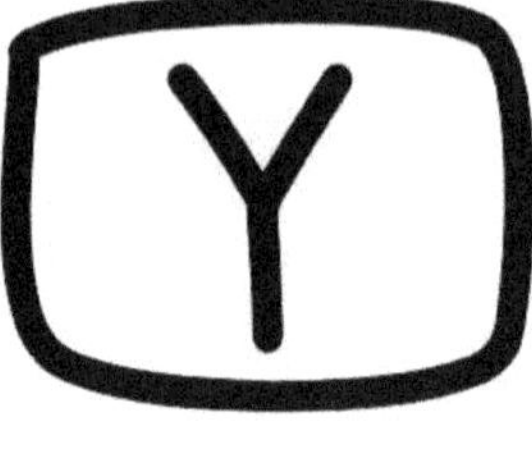

Concept - Letters Revision

Match The Letters With The Images Beginning With The Letter Sound.

V

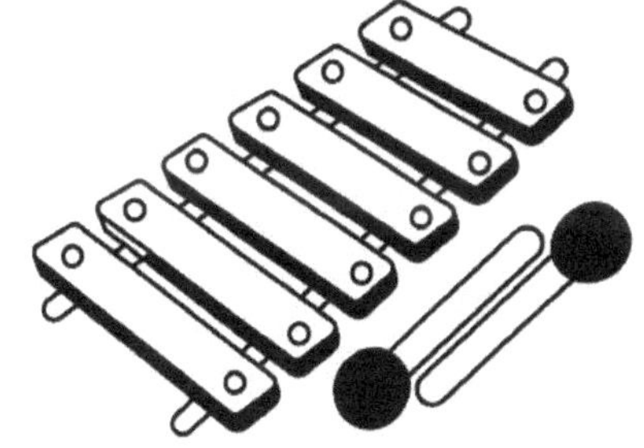

W

X

Y

Let's Learn Letter Y

Date:________

Color letter Y

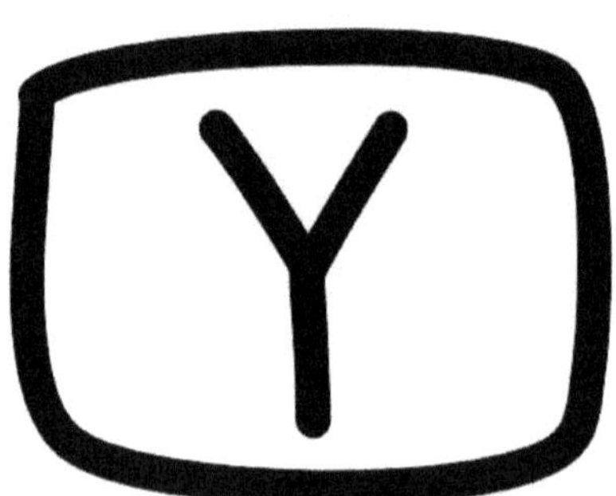

Color the Yam

X

X

Y

Y

Y

Y

Y

Find and color the images starting from letter Y

78

Concept - Letter Z

Find And Color Letter Z

Concept - Letters Revision

Match The Letters With The Images Beginning With The Letter Sound.

W

X

Y

Z

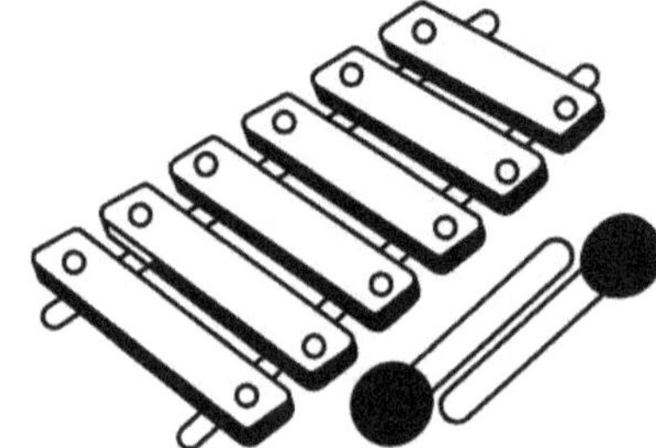

80

Let's Learn Letter Z Date:________

Color letter Z

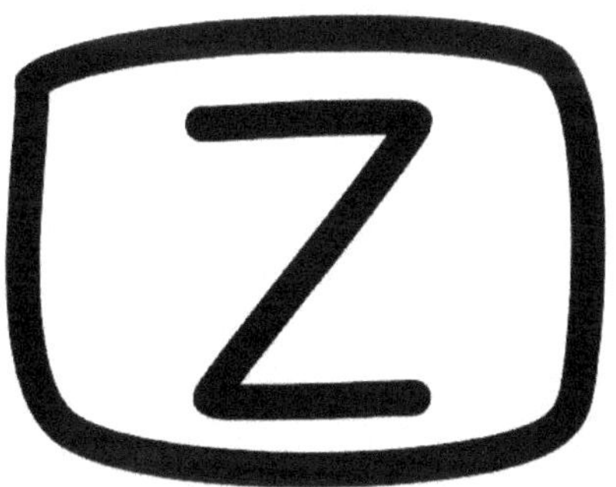

Color the Zucchini

Find and circle the letter Z

Y Z Y Z

Z Z Z Z

Find and color the images starting from letter Z

Revision Of Letters Till Z

Stick A Sound To Match The beginning Sound Of The Given Objects.

Stick A Sound To Match The beginning Sound Of The Given Objects.

Revision Of Letters Till Z

Stick A Sound To Match The beginning Sound Of The Given Objects.

Revision Of Letters Till Z

Stick A Sound To Match The beginning Sound Of The Given Objects.